Fitzbillies

STORIES & RECIPES
FROM A 100-YEAR-OLD
CAMBRIDGE BAKERY

TIM HAYWARD & ALISON WRIGHT

With recipes by:

GILL ABBS

PAUL WHITE

STUART HUTCHINSON

Photography by SAM A. HARRIS

Hardie Grant

QUADRILLE

DEDICATION

TO OUR CUSTOMERS PAST, PRESENT AND FUTURE
Thanks very much for coming; please come again soon.

TO OUR STAFF, PAST, PRESENT AND FUTURE
If it wasn't for you, none of this would happen.

TO OUR LANDLORDS, SUPPLIERS AND BUSINESS PARTNERS
Thanks for your support and goodwill.

TO OUR FRIENDS AND FAMILY, ESPECIALLY LIBERTY
Thanks for listening to us talk about nothing but
Fitzbillies for eight years now, and probably a good few more to come.

CONTENTS

Introduction

Fitzbillies is a 100-year-old cake shop, café and bakery in the centre of the historic city of Cambridge. Although that makes us quite old by the standards of most businesses, a century is actually pretty young around here — some of the colleges date back 800 years. Though we're one of the youngest institutions in this beautiful place, we like to think we're firmly at its heart.

The bakery was founded by a couple of local boys on their return from the First World War. Back then, before the appearance of fast food and ready meals, if students didn't want to eat in the full formality of a college dining room, there were only small local independent shops to serve them. Perhaps some hot soup or stew from the pub, or a cold pie or slice of ham from the butcher. Mainly, though, there was 'tea and cake', served to students by the likes of The Whim, the Copper Kettle and, most famous and beloved of all, Fitzbillies.

Fitzbillies was not a 'patisserie' with fussy, aspirational confections; it didn't do 'Viennoiserie', rich with butter and accompanied by coffee. It offered a uniquely British kind of baking. Simple, familiar... not a million miles away from what mother might have cooked at home and loved equally by children, adults, working men and women, undergraduates, dons, divines and aristocrats. This kind of cake shop was a vital part of every small town, feeding everyone the treats they loved.

Our illustrious alumni

Of course, as part of the Cambridge story, Fitzbillies is also a destination for tourists and every year we serve thousands of people from all over the world. It's a strange thought. The café is pretty, but not as gorgeous as the old college buildings; it's old, but not as old as the institutions around it. Maybe, like us, our guests just want to sit, eat cake and absorb the unique atmosphere of the place.

Sometimes we see an advert on the television featuring a celebrity endorsement. You know the kind of thing — a footballer tells everybody how good a particular kind of crisp is — and so we started listing the people who've loved our cakes. The people who conquered Everest, discovered DNA and the proton, wrote brief histories of time, the inventors of webcams, microcomputers and atom bombs, creators of radio telescopes and members of supergroups, actors, archbishops... the occasional spy... and Stephen Fry.

To be honest, the list is so long and so brilliant that we can't even begin to write it down. We've lost count of the many sparkling and influential people who have sat on our rickety chairs. So many essays and theses have been finished on our tables. Sure, there are glossier, more fashionable and modern bakeries, but we're quietly confident that more of our customers have been Nobel Prize winners than any other bakery in the world.

Open to all

Proud though we are of our history, it's not the best part. Sitting in the café, we watch thousands of stories unfold. A builder walks in to buy sausage rolls for lunch and falls into conversation with the guy from the tech startup who's also buying them for his team lunch. There are a couple of oarsmen from the Cambridge Blue Boat sitting in the coffee shop, which always flusters the baristas. There's an elderly couple who've come in every Wednesday since they retired. There are always young couples studying together, flirting or breaking up, and old couples popping by to reminisce about when they did exactly the same thing. During interview weeks, we see nervous young applicants brought in by their far more nervous parents. Over the next three years the lucky ones will be back dozens more times, sometimes with books, a new boyfriend or their tutor for an informal supervision, and, if all goes well, the whole family will be back in on Graduation Day. Many return to college to get married and we're proud to make their wedding cakes. Perhaps the best thing is when people who've spent particularly happy times here bring in their babies or children and it feels like all of this will go on and on forever. It may sound strange, but to us, and our regulars, we're a 'neighbourhood café' even if it's for a particularly special little neighbourhood, a sort of 'family favourite', even when that family is now dispersed all over the globe.

This is the tradition that Fitzbillies has continued, unbroken to the present day. Simple British baking in an entirely democratic environment, serving sticky buns and sausage rolls to dustmen and dons alike. Since the last Lyons Tea Shop shut its doors, we've been amongst the few surviving carriers of that torch – making people happy with tea, cake and hospitality.

This book will take you into the unique world of Fitzbillies. The work of the bakers, their recipes and techniques, alongside our history and the story of how we turned the business around. We'll hear the stories of some of our amazing customers, tales from our special corner of authentic British baking and you'll learn how you too can make people happy with tea and cake.

Taking on Fitzbillies

The latest chapter in the history of Fitzbillies began on 9 February 2011 when we first read that it had gone bankrupt and closed down. Tim kept a diary from that day through to our reopening. Now, with the benefit of hindsight and eight years' experience, it's interesting to look back on the combination of naivety and determination that saw us through.

Notes from Tim's diary

It must have appeared simultaneously on my laptop in a coffee shop where I was putting the final gloss on a piece for the *Guardian* and on Alison's desk in the marketing company where she was working. I was quietly doing my job, writing about food, and she was doing hers, relaunching and guiding big corporate brands.

It was a tweet from @stephenfry, comedian and famed alumnus of Cambridge University, who posted:

> 'No! No! Say it ain't so – not Fitzbillies? Why I tweeted a pic of one of their peerless Chelsea buns but a sixmonth ago.'

9 February 2011

I'd had some experience in catering. I'd spent a chunk of my youth working in kitchens in seaside towns in the UK, and in diners and dives in the US. But that was decades ago. Al had grown up in Cambridge. Her 21st birthday cake – a vast *croquembouche* – had been ordered from Fitzbillies and, like Stephen Fry, she knew the place as a Cambridge institution, a tea shop and bakery that prided itself on selling generations of students the world's stickiest Chelsea buns. Now, when we followed the link to the local paper at the bottom of the tweet, we saw that recession had driven it into bankruptcy and it had shut its doors.

'Did you see the tweet?'

'I did. Terribly sad. Awful how places like that are going…'

'I've called the agents. We're going to view it on Monday.'

These days, when we think of bankruptcy, we tend to imagine large companies or even small countries cutting up their credit cards in an organised way. The reality for thousands of high-street businesses is more depressing, more human and more brutally ugly. When the bailiffs arrived at Fitzbillies, they asked the customers to leave, gave the staff a few minutes to assemble their personal possessions and hand over their keys and led them out of the building. The shop was still full of food, the bakery full of half-baked cakes and mixer bowls full of flour. The landlords subsequently cleared the place well, but when we arrived just weeks later, it was dark, filthy and unloved.

But it was also apparent that over the years the business had been contracting inside its shell. Sure, the cake shop was still out front, but everything behind it had suffered from a lack

of cash. Equipment hadn't been maintained, staff hadn't been paid and, justifiably lacking motivation, they had let everything slip. Sections that couldn't be made to work had just been closed down and forgotten, meaning that around 75% of the floor space of the building was unused. The place was a disaster area, but to Al it was still Fitzbillies, it still had the bones... the spirit of a lovely old business – and it couldn't be left to die.

A large local estate agency had been appointed to handle the reassignment of the lease by the landlords, Pembroke College. The business itself, its equipment, goodwill and, as we were about to discover, its name, were in the hands of the Official Receiver. I have to admit, with some experience of the industry, that the idea of fighting to pick up the pieces of a business that had been on the slide for years, on a provincial high street and on the precipice of a recession seemed ridiculous, but Al's enthusiasm was so consuming I wanted to support it. There were, after all, around 200 separate individuals and organisations expressing an interest that we had almost no chance of getting through, and in truth, it seemed better for us both to let the natural course of things crush this crazy idea rather than me.

We lashed together a document expressing interest. To be fair, once we'd set down Al's experience in marketing, her connection to the town, my profile as a food writer and some entirely speculative figures, the idea didn't look quite as absurd as I'd thought, but after we sealed the envelope and dropped it in a post box, I tried to get back to real work.

I was still conflicted, I must admit. In terms of the state of the high street and of the catering industry, this couldn't be a worse time and yet I'd spent the last few years, like most British food writers, banging on about rediscovering our food culture, about how independent food businesses were being driven out of the high street, about the importance of good food from basic ingredients in everyday life rather than three-star restaurants. Suddenly here was a chance to do something about it.

22 February 2011

Al called. 'We're down to the last four candidates. We've got about a fortnight to get a full business plan together.'

I was in something like shock. There was now a 25% chance that the entire framework of our family's world was going to be voluntarily collapsed into something that Al saw as an unalloyed good but for me looked insanely risky: it's a bankrupt cake shop for chrissake. What am I going to do? Commute to bloody Cambridge every day to make buns?

The next fortnight was frenzied. The first call was to friends and contacts. Thomas Blythe, General Manager at the St. John restaurant group, is a great friend who has 'worked every station' in the catering world. He sat at the dining table and dictated nonstop for an hour the astonishing list of things we'd have to think about. Laundry, staff training, blasting out grease traps, deliveries, premises licences, recycling, till systems, insurance, late-night fridge emergencies, visits from the Environmental Health Officer and taking credit cards. Next in was Gerry Moss, career baker and now head of operations at Gail's. Gerry's list included shop layouts, display, coffee machines, bakery equipment, stock control, uniforms and a couple of hundred other things to consider on the retail and bakery sides of the operation. Next was Dan Hopwood, interior designer and, most usefully, a trained architect.

There were some technical issues, but within minutes Dan was sketching out ways the space could be opened, lightened and made functional.

The business plan started to take shape. I'm not great with money but Al is. I've also known her long enough to be sure that her parameters of operation are conservative. If she said we could make this work financially, we could.

With Dan's brilliant designs and an idea of the building costs, together with all the information we'd gleaned from Thomas and Gerry, Alison had created a paper model of the business that looked like it could actually happen. It was then that the realisation began to creep up on us that there was no way we'd be able to do this from a distance. We'd need to be on site all day every day. We also realised that if we let our London house and rented in Cambridge, we'd have enough surplus income to buffer the first crucial years of the new business. Suddenly, it looked like we might be moving.

11 March 2011

We were led through the imposing arches of Pembroke College for an interview with the Bursar, Chris Blencowe, who was responsible for running the 700-year-old college and its estates. Al was armed with beautifully bound and illustrated business plans. I carried a monumental Bakewell tart she'd baked that morning. Chris and his team went at the business plan like a pack of management consultants, but in the end, perhaps swayed by the Bakewell, they smiled.

Now every available waking moment was spent on the project. For Al, it simply meant packing two and a half jobs into her already ridiculous schedule. Dan, the interior designer, was a godsend, generating a new drawing

to represent every bonkers whim. The local planning authority had to clear each change to the building's interior and everything had to be backed up by accurate drawings. Meanwhile, we were deep in negotiation with the Official Receiver. The previous owner had finally got around to registering the company about eight months before going bust. This meant that although the shopfront, which under planning law couldn't be changed, featured a huge carved gilt 'Fitzbillies', we couldn't actually trade under that name without buying it back from the Receiver. We were also buying the fittings of the bakery – knackered fridges, elderly proving cabinets, a huge industrial rolling machine and an oven that was too big to be moved out of the building.

Nobody else was particularly interested in bidding for the equipment – so many high-street bakers go out of business every year that you can always pick up the kit on eBay for little more than the transport cost – but several people had caught on to the importance of the Fitzbillies name. A small and surreal bidding war developed as we tried to reunite the building with the name it had traded under since 1920.

There was also the vexed matter of the secret recipe for the Chelsea bun. Apparently it wasn't part of the deal with the Receiver, but remained in the head of the ex-head baker Gill Abbs, who, with 40 years of experience cooking the 50 or so lines of baked goods in the shop window, had been snapped up by a big local commercial bakery after the bankruptcy. Unless we could do something about recovering the traditional recipes, we were going to be selling cupcakes. Luckily for us, after a little negotiation, Gill was soon back in her old job.

I started thinking about menus for savoury food. We could use the space behind the shop to run a traditional tea room, but that by itself would be economic suicide. Traditional teas are massively labour intensive and you can't charge much for them. Our research kept turning up comments that 'there's nowhere decent to eat in Cambridge'. I found that difficult to understand, but then Cambridge isn't an ordinary town. The academics — those with much of the disposable income and inclination to eat out — eat fantastically high-quality food from their own college kitchens. There are plenty of chain joints catering to students and their visiting parents, but Cambridge had been named 'Clone Town' a couple of years before when researchers discovered that there were more chains per head of population than anywhere else in the UK. That accusation obviously hurt. It kept coming up in our meetings with Pembroke, interviews with potential customers and conversations with local businesses.

We needed to run a proper lunch service — and eventually dinner too — in order to make the place work financially. We'd have to insert a savoury kitchen into the bakery, but we'd also need to choose our food carefully. The town wanted Fitzbillies to feel 'non-chain', the students needed it to be affordable, I wanted it to be British in tradition and the brand demanded it should fit in with the original feel of the bakery. I started jotting down lists of pies, big roasts done slowly in the dying heat of the baker's oven, soups and savouries. It was fun. Unlike arguing with the council about drain lines or the interminable bloody discussion about which of 42 shades of white the walls should be, this was something I felt I could do well. But the last time I'd put on whites and

bellied up to the range was 28 years and four stone ago. I couldn't run a kitchen any more — we were going to need a chef.

Gerry and Thomas came with us to visit the site again as we planned layouts, positions for waiter stations and where the kitchen kit would fit. Thomas brought along an old friend, Rosie Sykes, a phenomenal chef and food writer who was well advanced with her own secret project for a restaurant in Cambridge. Rosie had trained with Joyce Molyneux at The Carved Angel, and worked with Shaun Hill, Alastair Little and Margot Henderson as well as at half a dozen other astonishingly good British restaurants. She's firmly of the tradition of British cooking using local ingredients, and her low-key personal style we recognised as ideal for running a kitchen that was squeezed into an existing traditional bakery. Al and I knew we were going to have trouble attracting a good chef.

6 June 2011

The date Al handed in her notice was, remarkably appropriately, also the anniversary of D-Day. The first viewings from potential tenants indicated that we'd be able to let our London house for good money. All of which meant I could clear my head for the building work. I'd tackled several medium-sized projects — we'd done up a couple of houses from wrecks — but this was going to be the biggest job I'd undertaken by a long way. There is, though, one universal truth about building projects of any size. If you're on the site, you'll save money. Partly because you can make yourself useful with odd cleaning or labouring duties, which helps to distract the builders from the fact that you're watching everyone like a particularly avaricious hawk. And if a part or material suddenly isn't where it's needed, you don't lose a whole day of a tradesman's time — you just get in the car and go buy the thing. But above all, decisions are made on the spot. You don't come back in three days to find a wall has been erected a few inches too close to the loo door — you'll be there when they start, so you can make sure it's right.

Al came up to the site for a day, and as we wandered through the rubble, her phone beeped. It was the automatic alert she'd set up on the property search site. Almost incredibly there was an actual family house up for rent in central Cambridge. We'd been looking for weeks, and in a town where the colleges and big tech firms snap up most available family rentals for their own people, it had felt like nothing suitable would ever come up. We wanted to be close to the shop and to Liberty's new school — she'd got into the same school her mum went to, which pleased her no end. Two phone calls later, still covered in cement dust, I was standing in the hall of a beautiful house just around the corner and overlooking the school gate. It was perfect; a beautiful, really comfortable family home — just what we were all going to need as a safe base over the next insane year. With the house and school sorted, the building on time and on budget, all we needed now was a chef…

A couple of weeks later, on my 47th birthday (or maybe 48th), Thomas dropped by again to see how everything was going. 'You should talk to Rosie,' he said, 'I think she's being messed around on her project. You could be good for each other.' It was an almost unbelievable stroke of luck that Rosie was able to join us.

We're very alike in almost all the things we believe about eating out in the UK, but Rosie has the added reputation for launching outstanding kitchens. She asked if we'd also consider hiring Tim, a soft-spoken south

Londoner with Robert Smith hair and a legendary hand with terrines and pâtés. His most recent gig had been at the renowned Anchor & Hope in Southwark. Rosie had planned to have Tim with her on her project, and though we'd only have him for a month, he'd turn out to be a solid asset.

A couple of days later, I was screwing on the new table tops when Jack van Praag walked in off the street. He liked the look of the place, he said, and wondered if he might come and do a few shifts in the kitchen between his new childcare commitments. I was at first perhaps a little reticent. 'Do you have much experience?' I asked. 'I used to run my own place, went travelling, worked at Rose Bakery in Paris and Chez Panisse.' I put down my screwdriver to shake hands… it looked like we might have a full kitchen team for opening.

At the bakery the final touches were being put to the construction work. I built the big bar to hold the coffee machine. I suspected Al didn't entirely agree with my desire for a 'state-of-the-art' coffee counter, but then she drinks herbal tea and pretends to like it. I might have happily left The Big Smoke for this bike-infested heritage play-park, but I was sure as hell bringing the best bits with me. My new workplace was going to feature the sort of coffee that would put Shoreditch to shame.

We set up a space to interview new staff. Most food businesses complain that it's tough to find good people outside of the big cities. I can't say I agree. We were lucky, I know. Kirsty had been the head waitress at the old Fitzbillies and she was a revelation. A superbly talented catering professional who'd been crushed when the business went under, her knowledge of the local audience, contacts, ideas and her calm brilliance in a crisis were the sort of assets you

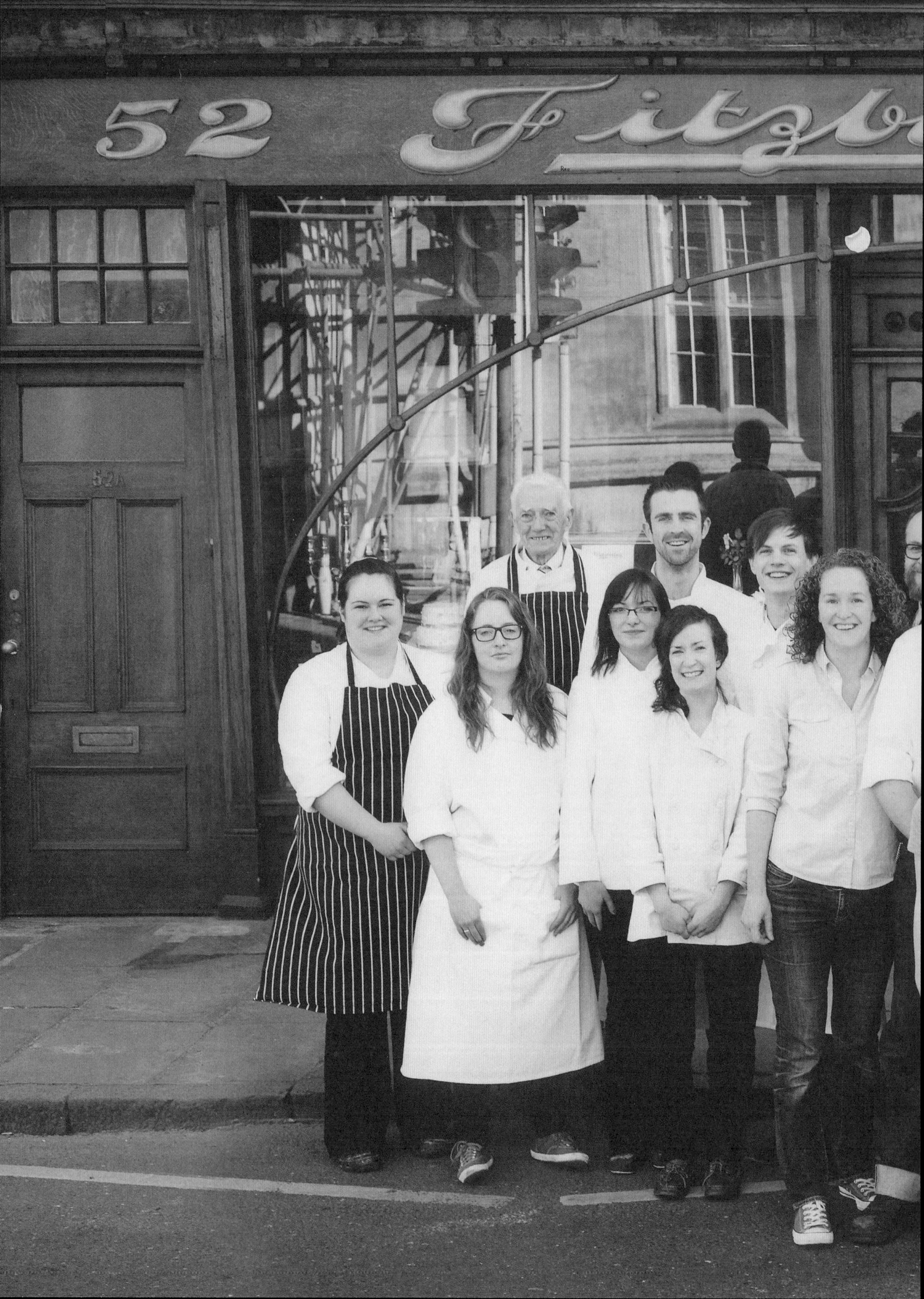
52

wouldn't find in some of the best London crews. She also loved Fitzbillies in a way that reinforced our feeling that we were just the current fortunate caretakers of an immortal institution.

Others arrived in response to ads in the window. Caz, Stuart, Whitney, Holly, Fiona, Tom, Lucy, Issy and Abbi ranged from first-class front-of-house people to first-job school-leavers, but all came with a love of food and real enthusiasm for Fitzbillies.

One Wednesday I was working on the plumbing when a tall, slim gentleman in a flat cap with military bearing walked in. He sat with Al in the kitchen and they talked for an hour, pouring over some books he'd brought. 'Who was that?' I asked. According to the last owners, 'Old Tom' sort of 'comes with the place'. He was an ex-paratrooper who had trained in the kitchens of the big London hotels after the war and had been at Fitzbillies on and off ever since. He'd survived three sets of owners, was around 85 years old (he said he'd stopped counting) and decorated cakes with heartbreaking beauty.

'I feel like he just interviewed me,' said Al. He agreed to fill in a time sheet, but could set his own hours. Within days he was in the kitchen, swinging trays of buns and huge 25kg drums of syrup into stacks like two men half his age.

19 August 2011

The new staff arrived and began a thorough clean as the builders packed up and retreated. The false wall protecting the kitchen came down and, after a 5.30am start, I gleefully joined in the loading of the very last skip. Every restaurateur I've asked tells the same story about opening day – driving the builders out the back door as the first customers come in through the front. Fitzbillies, it seemed, was alive again.

The first trays of hot Chelsea buns began flying out of the cleaned and renovated ovens as Rosie turned out 'sample' food that would make an angel weep. I wondered if the builders had any idea where the hands that built their bacon sandwich had worked.

On Thursday night we rolled home late. The next day, we began a three-day 'Chelsea bun Weekend'. The tills weren't working, and we weren't up to speed in the bakery, but the plan was to turn out buns and tea to the people of Cambridge for a few days, just to say thanks and to get the team working well together. We'd all muck in to serve, give guided tours of the bakery and generally be lovely to everyone. The doors would open at 10.00. At 09.30 they were already queueing along the street and around the corner…

The day after that

While you're setting up a business, opening day is the target, the end goal, what you plan for. But, of course, it is just the beginning. You wake up the next day and do it again and, in the case of Fitzbillies, you do it again every day (except Christmas Day and New Year's Day) all year round. And the next year, and the one after. Getting Fitzbillies open again was a great achievement, but it had a long way to go. While the standard of the baking was always good, thanks to Gill, in other ways we were rank amateurs. We adopted the approach, which we still maintain, of just trying to make things better day by day. Spotting the next problem and solving it. Hiring people who can help us do that.

Fitzbillies Bridge Street

By January 2015, we were three and a half years into our new life and our new business. The café was ever-more popular, with queues at the door every weekend. While every day was still unpredictable, it felt like we could just about take a breath. Time for the next project then…

We cycle to Fitzbillies through the centre of Cambridge. One day we noticed that a beautiful, double-fronted Victorian shop, right opposite Magdalene Bridge punt station, was up for rent. We knew instantly that it should be our next branch – it was the other end of town from Trumpington Street, a busy street and miles from the nearest decent cup of coffee. It took over a year to persuade St John's College that we were the right tenants and to get the change of use from shop to café, but eventually, in May 2016, Fitzbillies Bridge Street opened its doors.

It's a coffee shop really, smaller than the original branch, and was initially supplied with cakes, pastries and all the makings of brunch from the Trumpington Street kitchen and bakery. It was a success from day one and with that success came a new set of challenges. Production capacity. It was around this time that we stopped serving dinner at Fitzbillies Trumpington Street in order to concentrate on the ever-busier daytime trade, and we also started thinking seriously about moving the bakery offsite to give the bakers more room and to fulfil our ambition to make our own bread.

A new bakery

We searched long and hard for suitable premises to relocate our bakery. We needed a big space, very close to central Cambridge in order to get the Chelsea buns and other cakes to the two branches quickly first thing in the morning and so that our bakers could get to work by bike. Before we found one, we heard that Cobs Bakery, the long-time supplier of the delicious white baps we use for our bacon rolls, was going to close. We couldn't bear the loss of the baps and it gave us a ready-made opportunity to start producing all of our own bread, so Cobs joined the Fitzbillies family in July 2018, with Tim's brother Matt as our first delivery driver.

By that summer, with Trumpington Street and Bridge Street getting busier and busier, the need for a bigger bakery for our cake bakers became pressing. Eventually we found a lovely, light, modern space close to the railway station that was big enough for the Cobs bread bakers and the cake bakers. And in December 2018, with only one day's break in the Chelsea bun production, all the bakers moved into their new home.

Looking forward

We write this in May 2019, looking back at nearly eight years of work at Fitzbillies. Eight years of constant improvement, just trying to do better every day. Making more delicious food, making more customers happy (most of the time), creating more jobs, keeping the institution going. Of course we wish we'd known then what we know now. We would still have done it, but we're not sure we'd have the energy to do it again!

The next thing is to do justice to our 100th birthday in 2020. A vanishingly small percentage of companies live to be 100. A business-school textbook will tell you that it takes changing with the times, being prepared to adapt to survive. We believe we've done that while staying true to what made Fitzbillies beloved from the start – bloody good cake… and buns and coffee and brunch. The day we forget that, we know our customers will remind us.

A history of Fitzbillies

An advertisement in the *Cambridge News* tells us that Fitzbillies first opened its doors to customers on Monday, 4 October 1920. The date was no coincidence – it was the first Monday of the university term. And then, just as now, the owners would have known that they needed to be ready for this busy time of year.

Ernest and Arthur Mason founded Fitzbillies, using their demob money from the First World War to set up a confectioner's at 52 Trumpington Street – their initials are still visible in worn-out gold letters on the shopfront. They were the sons of local character 'Ticker' Mason, who had a baker's shop further up Trumpington Street, at number 41. The nickname 'Ticker' came from his custom of wearing an unusually loud pocket watch.

A small businessman with entrepreneurial spirit and making mainly bread, it was perhaps Ticker who spotted the opportunity and encouraged his sons to open a confectioner's – a complementary business specialising in fancy cakes and pastries.

FITZBILLIES (Confectioners),
52, Trumpington Street, Cambridge.

We Beg to Announce that this Establishment
WILL OPEN on OCTOBER 4th, inst.
E. & A. MASON.

The beginning

Ernest and Arthur had the shopfront designed in the unusual Belgian Art Nouveau style that remains today. Perhaps they had seen this style when they were in Flanders during the war. It certainly contributed to the 'high-class' look and appeal of the business. The bakery was through the back of the shop, taking up the whole of the yard in the middle of the block. It had a huge brick oven with a tall chimney that remained in use until the 1980s.

Ernest and his wife Phyllis lived above the business. 'Phil', as she was known, ran the shop and we are told that 'she was the one they were all scared of'. Ernest and Arthur's sisters, Maud, May and Doll, helped in the shop from time to time.

Fitzbillies quickly became the cake shop of choice for the university and town. It produced the full selection of buns, pastries, savouries and fancy cakes you would have found in any high-street confectioner's of the time. In the early days it was even more famous for the special Fitzbillies sponge cake than for the Chelsea buns.

Philomena Guillebaud, a long-time resident of Cambridge and regular customer of Fitzbillies throughout her life, reminisced:

'I was born in Cambridge in 1926, in a don's family. Before the Second World War, no don's family tea table would have been complete without a Fitzbillies' sponge cake, it was THE THING for which Fitzbillies was famous. Chelsea buns – and Bath buns – and what we called candlegrease buns – were on offer, but it was the cake that carried the flag. And it was very good, and it was often preceded at the tea table by cucumber sandwiches on brown bread with the crusts cut off. Apparently the cake was never made again after the Second World War, perhaps because of rationing.

'Here is the recipe. I got it from my sister, who got it from our mother, who got it (as a very very special favour) from the lady who ran Fitzbillies at the time, whose name my sister thinks was Mrs Mason. My sister remembers her as a rather grim-visaged lady, but our mother, who was known to be a good cook, evidently charmed her out of the recipe, which was otherwise a secret.

'Don't ask me for any clarifications, what I have given below is the verbatim text and is all we know.

> 8 eggs
> 8oz sugar
> 7oz flour
> 1 tsp pounded tangerine peel

Separate eggs, beat yolks and sugar till creamy, fold in beaten egg whites.
Sprinkle tangerine and flour at the same time.
Line a greased tin with fine breadcrumbs.
Bake in a very low oven for about 1½ hours.'

THE FITZBILLIES NAME

We are often asked why Fitzbillies is called Fitzbillies. The short answer is that it is a diminutive of Fitzwilliam, named after The Fitzwilliam Museum just down the road — but the long answer is more entertaining.

We know that Ernest and Arthur Mason originally wanted to call the business Fitzwilliam's or Fitzwilliam Bakery. So why didn't they? One story is that The Fitzwilliam Museum refused them permission; another that there was already a Fitzwilliam Bakery in Ireland, so they were unable to trademark the name.

Why Fitzbillies? Newspaper articles from the time refer to the fact that undergraduates irreverently called The Fitzwilliam Museum the 'Fitzbilly Gallery'. And the motto of the rowing crew of Fitzwilliam College, then called Fitzwilliam House and situated on Trumpington Street, was and to this day still is, rather stirringly, 'For Fitzbilly Pride'.

More scandalously, the original Viscount Fitzwilliam of Merrion, the benefactor of the museum, had two illegitimate sons whom he called Fitz and Billie. The historian of The Fitzwilliam Museum suggested Fitzbillies was named after them.

There is also a glacier in Svarlbard in Norway called the Fitzbilly Glacier or Fitzbillybreen. For a while, we were hopeful that it had been discovered and named after the shop by a true bun lover. However, we have to concede that it was actually named after Fitzwilliam College by one of the Cambridge men on expeditions to Norway in the 1920s and 30s.

'GOING DOWN' FOR THE LAST TIME

By A Cambridge Woman

'We feel suddenly we must pack into these last days everything that we have most enjoyed. We must picnic up the river beyond Grantchester, where the stream runs slow and you can bathe. We must tramp once more over the Gog and Magog hills and find the Roman road that still runs as straight as the legions planned it. We must defy authority and spend a June night in the college orchard in hammocks slung precariously from baby apple trees. We must eat slabs and slabs of "Fitzbilly" cake – surely the most luscious sponge cake in the world and known only to a Cambridge baker.'

The Daily Mail
Wednesday, 5 June, 1929

The Second World War & rationing

The Second World War was a particularly challenging time for the business. Bakers and confectioners, like other catering businesses, had to apply to the Ministry of Food for their quota of ingredients. The allocations were usually well calculated, but nevertheless a trade grew up where businesses bartered with each other to get what they needed.

One of the bakers who came to barter ingredients during the war was Wilfred Day. He had a bakery business in Willingham, just outside Cambridge. He brought his son Garth with him, who was then in his teens. Garth told his father that when he was older he wanted to run Fitzbillies. Mr Day mentioned to the Masons that if they ever wanted to sell, he would like to have first refusal.

Although ingredients were in short supply during and after the war, demand for Chelsea buns was higher than ever. Customers now in their 90s have told us stories of their experiences as undergraduates in the late 1940s and early '50s. The food in colleges was terrible and meagre. A Chelsea bun was a huge luxury and the Masons must have wanted to make sure that the few buns available went to regular customers. So, the only way to get a Chelsea bun was to bring back the bag from your previous bun. It was a lucky undergraduate indeed who, on going to his new rooms at the beginning of term in October, found that the previous inhabitant had left him his Fitzbillies bag.

'When the war was over, everyone thought food queues would be over, too. In fact, everything continued as greyly as before, and the most anxious queues I had ever joined were outside Fitzbillies in Cambridge. No undergraduate tea party was complete without their Chelsea Buns, syrupy, well spiced, licentious and exceptional during the years of ersatz cakes and shortages. I still think they are the best Chelsea Buns I have ever eaten.'

The Observer Guide to British Cookery by Jane Grigson

The next owners

Meanwhile, Garth Day grew up, joined the army and fought in Sicily. When he was demobbed in 1946 he went to the National Bakery School at Borough Polytechnic Institute, winning the Renshaw Cup for Confectionery. After leaving college he married Annette and they went into business in Aldeburgh. Then one day in 1958 he got a phone call from his father. The Masons had remembered his request and called to say they wanted to sell Fitzbillies.

Garth and Annette dropped everything and moved to Cambridge, bringing with them two long-serving members of staff: Malcolm Grayling who worked in the bakery and Yvonne who worked

Wilfrid R Wood 32.

in the shop. Mr Day ran the bakery and, as a particularly skilled cake decorator, did much of the decorating himself. Mrs Day ran the shop with a firm hand and installed a series of mirrors so she could check that customers were never left unattended and to maintain surveillance over the till.

Christopher Day, Garth and Annette's son, remembers his childhood growing up in the rooms above the shop in 52 Trumpington Street:

> 'We lived on the premises, downstairs in the kitchen under the shop; and bedrooms, bathroom and living rooms (i.e. posh bits used only on special days) on the first and second floors. Our play areas were the store (back rooms leading to a passage to Downing St) and the passage to the bakery.
>
> 'There was (what seemed to a small boy) a massive chimney above the oven at the back. In our time it was a stone oven, heated at 5 or 6 every morning. The first things to get baked were those which needed the hottest temperatures, followed by those needing gradually lower temperatures. Most of the bakery work was done by early afternoon, so the 'men' (which it was mostly) went home.
>
> 'My father fired the oven every day. Like a steel furnace, the stone would crack if it cooled too much, which would wreck the oven. There was a fuel tank for the burner for the oven, which was refilled by a hose from a tanker in Trumpington St. In retrospect it was rather surprising that the whole lot didn't go up in flames before it actually did.
>
> 'My father used to take the bakery staff on a one-day trip every year (equivalent of a works outing, I suppose) mostly to the seaside, although I remember at least one year they splashed out and flew abroad (Copenhagen?) for a couple of days. (I don't think similar benefits extended to the shop staff.) The whole business shut down for two weeks every August for summer holidays.'

Building a reputation

Christopher's sister, Patricia Birtles (née Day) remembers being set to work as a child and 'at the age of 12 being paid 12s 6d for 7.30am–2pm on a Maundy Thursday packing hot cross buns in bags of 6s and 12s'. There were queues outside the shop and round past what was then Heffers bookshop on the corner.

Fitzbillies' reputation was such that there were often long queues. There is a story that during the Cold War, *Pravda* ran a feature under a picture of the long lines queuing for Chelsea buns outside Fitzbillies claiming that even the affluent Westerners were forced to queue for bread.

It is also said that Edmund Hillary ordered a crate of Chelsea buns as part of the rations for his ascent of Everest. It seems likely that the high fat and sugar content would have assured their survival at Base Camp, but we are still searching for hard evidence.

Tom Whitehead started work at Fitzbillies in 1962 and gave a detailed account of how the business worked in those days:

> 'At the back of the bakery was the old-fashioned side flue oven. A giant thing like a bunsen burner the size of a cannon. It heated a huge hot water tank as well.
>
> 'The production was scheduled for the oven. Mr Day started at 6am to get the doughs ready. Then the oven was switched off and cleaned. Then the first firing went in. Sausage rolls, pies, meat products, bread, Chelsea buns, all in particular layers. When that came out it went straight into the shop when it opened at 8.30 to be served hot.
>
> 'The bakers worked eight hours a day, five days a week and five hours on Saturdays at double time. The business was geared to term. As soon as term ended, production went down about 40 or 50%.
>
> 'The Chelsea buns were the big thing. Mr Day would only make to the capacity of the ove: 66 buns on a tray, then four loads on a weekday, seven on a Saturday. Mrs Day had a cast-iron control on the shop. Anything slapdash it went straight back.
>
> 'In the second firing we baked all the small stuff: seven or eight trays of Norwegian crisps, Danish pastries, lemon meringue pie three days a week. Then there was a half-hour stop for breakfast at 9.45 or 10am. Then we made all the cakes, different flavours and decorations, on different days of the week. Monday was plain cakes, Tuesday chocolate cakes and chocolate roll, Wednesday tennis cakes, Thursday ginger roll, and so it went on.'

Fitzbillies continued under the successful ownership of the Days until 1980, when Mr and Mrs Day decided to retire. They sold the business to Clive and Julia Pledger, then newly engaged. The new owners approached Fitzbillies with true 1980s spirit, starting to make chocolates in 1983 and developing a mail-order business.

Tougher times

In 1984 they opened an in-store shop at Eaden Lilley, the department store that then took up most of Market Street, and another Fitzbillies branch in Regent Street. The *Cambridge Evening News* reported that they had plans to make the business a national chain, but reassured its readers: 'One thing that will not change if expansion takes place is the company's distinctive name.' But in the mid-8os, Fitzbillies' fortunes started to turn – there was now much more competition with cheaper mass-produced cakes available from supermarkets and an increasing number of fast-food options for students. By 1988, the Regent Street premises were put up for sale, as the owners decided to consolidate the business in the original Trumpington Street premises, and then in April 1991 Fitzbillies went into receivership for the first time.

There was considerable competition to buy the business out of receivership and it went to Penny Thompson, who had been a customer of the business for 20 years and fell in love with it while working there.

She got the business back on its feet and opened the first tea room at Trumpington Street on the first floor, above the shop. In 1998 she launched a website, selling Chelsea buns to customers all over the world. On the first day there were two orders: one from Australia, one from America.

The fire

Undoubtedly the worst moment in Fitzbillies' 100-year history occurred on the night of 21 December 1998 when a painter and decorator who had previously worked at Fitzbillies went on a burglary spree through Cambridge, starting at Fitzbillies, moving on to student accommodation in Trumpington Street and then breaking into a newsagent before being caught fleeing the scene by police. He had a bunch of 20 keys, including those for Fitzbillies. It was alleged that during the burglary, perhaps frustrated by not managing to break into the safe, he set fire to a roll of brown paper. He was, however, never convicted of arson.

Whichever way the fire started, Fitzbillies was almost destroyed. The entire building was gutted and the ones on each side completely blackened with smoke. The *Cambridge Evening News* reported that, 'at the height of the blaze, 35 firefighters from Cambridge, Cottenham, Sawston, Papworth and Swaffham Bulbeck battled thick smoke to fight the flames in the three-storey building in Trumpington Street. Efforts to tackle the fire were hampered by difficult access to pitched roofs at the rear of the building, which prevented crews from using ladders in the normal way, and by the collapse of the roof and internal floors.'

As soon as the buildings were declared safe, Old Tom went in to see what could be salvaged. The photos he took show a scene of total devastation. It must be one of the worst things any business owner can face.

Rebuilding Fitzbillies

Penny fought to keep the business alive. By October 1999, while work continued to rebuild 52 Trumpington Street, Fitzbillies opened a temporary shop next door at number 51 and started selling Chelsea buns again. The buns were baked by the Fitzbillies bakers, who were given workspace at Balzano's bakery in Cherry Hinton Road, a wonderful example of local businesses supporting each other in times of need. Everyone who loves Fitzbillies will always owe a debt of gratitude to Balzano's. Without them, it is doubtful the business could have kept going.

It took nearly two years to rebuild Fitzbillies, pretty much from the ground up. Pembroke College, the landlord, did a fine job building a new modern bakery at the back and restoring and recreating in painstaking detail the original design of the Art Nouveau shopfront. Eventually Fitzbillies reopened the cake shop at 52 Trumpington Street and next door, number 51, became the café/tea room.

Fitzbillies continued through the first decade of the new millennium, selling old favourites and adding new cakes to the range, but it faced more and tougher competition. In February 2011 the bailiffs knocked again…

'BARONESS FITZBILLIES'

Perhaps the greatest honour ever not quite paid to Fitzbillies was by the redoubtable Jean Barker, later Baroness Trumpington, a true Cambridge character from her days at Bletchley Park.

A former colleague of Baroness Trumpington wrote to *The Times* shortly after her death: 'There was another title that the then Jean Barker was contemplating when made a baroness. Shortly after her peerage was announced, I asked her what title she would take. She said: "I wanted to be Lady Fitzbillies, but they won't let me!"'

ICED CAKES

Layer Cakes	..	1/- & 2/- each
(Coffee, Orange, Strawberry, Walnut, Chocolate.)		
Cup Cakes	..	6d. & 1/- each
(Cherry, Ginger and Chocolate.)		
Special Jap Cake	..	1/6 each
Various Gateaux	..	from 1/- each
Oval Chocolate	..	2/- each

FRUIT CAKES

Cottage Cake	..	9d. each
H.M. Fruit ..	..	1/- each
Sultana Cakes	..	1/- & 2/- each
Madeira Cake	..	1/- & 1/9 each
Seed ,,	..	1/- each
Ginger Madeira	..	1/6 & 2/4 each
Date and Walnut	..	1/- each
Plain Ginger Bread	..	10d. each
Sultana ,,	..	1/- each
Genoa Cakes	..	1/6 & 2/2 each
Rich Fruit ..	..	1/9 & 3/6 each
Dundee	..	1/9 & 3/6 each

FRUIT SLAB

Mixed Fruit Slab ..	..	1/- per lb.
Sultana Loaf	..	1/- per lb.
Genoa Slab ..	..	1/6 per lb.
Cherry Slab	..	1/8 per lb.

Wedding Cake, 2/6 per lb.
Birthday Cakes made to order.

ICE BRICKS

Strawberry or Vanilla	..	3d., 6d. & 1/- each

Fresh Cream, 6d. per Carton.

W. H. & S.—86331

CONFECTIONERS

PRICE LIST

Fitzbillies Regd.

52 TRUMPINGTON STREET
CAMBRIDGE . TEL: 2500

FANCY BREAD

Milk Rolls	..	2d. & 4d. each
Brioche Rolls	..	2 for 1d.
Scotch Baps..	..	7 for 6d.
Wholemeal Rolls	..	2d. each
Soda Bread ..	..	4d. each

SCONES, etc.

Scones, Plain or Sultana	..	2 for 1d.
Wholemeal, Plain or Sultana	..	2 for 1d.
Currant Buns	..	2 for 1d.
,, ,,	..	7 for 6d.
Bun Rounds	..	4d. each
Currant Loaf	..	3d. each
Sultana ,,	..	4d. each
Sally Lunn ..	..	2d. & 4d. each
Muffins	..	1½d. each
Crumpets	..	8 for 6d.
Drop Scones	..	2 for 1d.
Swiss Buns	..	7 for 6d.
Bath ,,	..	,,
Rock ,,	..	,,
Doughnuts	..	,,
Chelsea Buns	..	1½d. each
Chocolate Ginger Buns	..	,,
Queen Cakes	..	
Currant, Plain, Chocolate, Ginger	..	7 for 6d.

PASTRIES

Almond Ring	..	1/3 each
Belgian Twists	..	1½d. each
Belgian Slices	..	,,
Almond Pastries	..	2d. each
Eccles Cakes	..	1½d. each
Palmier	..	7 for 6d.
Jam Tarts	..	1d. & 4d. each
Fruit Tarts, all flavours	..	6d. & 1/- each
Mince Pies	..	1½d., 6d. & 1/- each

SAVOURIES

Sausage Rolls	..	2d. each, 7 for 1/-
Beef Patties	..	2d., 6d. & 1/- each
Sausage Pies	..	6d. & 1/- each
Cornish Pasties	..	2d., 6d. & 1/- each
Fish Cakes ..	..	4d. each
Salmon Pies	..	6d. & 1/- each
Scotch Eggs	..	4½d. each
Pork Pies ..	..	3d. & 10d. each

Larger ones made to order.
As also Beef Steak Pies and Veal and Ham Pies.

FANCY CAKES

Biscuit Fancy Cakes	..	1½d. each
Shortbreads ..	..	½d. & 1d. each
Various Home-made Chocolate Biscuits	..	1d. each
Iced Fancy Cakes	..	2d. each, 7 for 1/-
Almond Macaroons	..	1d. each
Flap Jack	..	7 for 6d.
Crisps	..	½d. each
Parkins	..	,,
Meringue Fingers	..	7 for 6d.

FRESH CREAM GOODS

Devon Splits	..	2d. each
Eclairs	..	3d. each
Meringues	..	3d. each
Jam and Cream Sandwich	..	1/3 each
Brandy Creams	..	3d. each

SPONGE CAKES

Sponge Cakes	..	1½d. each
Sponge Loaf or Ring	..	8d. each
Swiss Rolls. Jam ..	..	6d. each
,, ,, Chocolate	..	,,
Sponge Sandwich ..	..	10d. ,,
H.M. ,,	..	6d. & 1/- each
Sponge Fingers	..	3/- per lb.
Special Fitzbillie Sponge	..	1/6 and 2/9 each

What to bake?

Most of the recipes in this book are the ones (or domestic versions of the ones) that we bake every day or several times a week in our bakery. We'd never counted and were surprised by how many different cakes, pastries and breads we actually make. We often wish we could be more efficient and bake more of fewer things, but this is the selection that answers most tastes at most different times of day. Of course, there are seasonal specials and weekend specials where we try out a new recipe to see what the customers think. But for something to make it permanently onto our cake list, something else has to go.

As soon as it had been announced that we were taking over Fitzbillies, it became clear that everyone who had ever been to the shop had a vested interest and, in their minds at least, a right to dictate what we should bake. There was never any doubt, of course, that we would make Chelsea buns. People enquired anxiously whether we had the original recipe. And we were able to assure them that Gill Abbs, the head baker who had been at Fitzbillies since 1971, would be rejoining the business, bringing with her the recipe and 40 years of Chelsea-bun-making expertise.

Everybody has a favourite

It's easy to think that Fitzbillies is all about the Chelsea buns. They account for about one third of all the baked goods that we sell. But there were always lots of other cakes, pastries and savouries and everyone had their favourites. Al's father was eager that we should make Norwegian crisps: a spiral of flaky pastry with currants and crisp caramel glaze, her mother keen that we make Florentines. Sandy, a gentleman of a certain age from Bury St Edmunds, used to telephone repeatedly to ask whether we were going to make coffee ripple cake. Others picked their way through the building site to tell us we must make Russian cake, tennis cake, Japonaise cake, ginger roll…

It became apparent early on that we had many expectations to meet and would struggle to satisfy everyone. To this day, eight years after reopening the business, most weeks someone will come in who may not have visited Cambridge or Fitzbillies for 20, 30, 40 or 50 years. Usually they are delighted to see the old shop in such good condition and obviously so popular, but equally we never know when they will express disgust and tell us off roundly because lardy cake is no longer available.

So, how did we decide what to bake when we reopened? In July 2011, soon after we had bought Fitzbillies out of receivership and while building work was going on upstairs, we started to sort through the basement of 51–52 Trumpington Street. It had been used as a mix of office and storeroom, and was filled with archaeological layers of everything from dirty chef's whites to silver, Art Deco tea pots. It took three whole days of sorting and removing bin bags of the less salubrious rubbish to get to the bottom of it, but when we did, we found a photocopy of an old Fitzbillies price list with a handwritten note from 1938.

The list becomes clear

We took that old list and a cake list that the previous owner, Penny Thompson, had kindly given us and sat down with Gill Abbs, the head baker, and Rosie Sykes, our opening head chef, to work out what we would make. What became clear to us quite quickly is that the same basic categories, corresponding to the same eating occasions and tastes, remained remarkably relevant. We needed Morning Goods or Daily Pastries for people on their way to work or to have with coffee; Iced Cakes for celebrations; Fancy Cakes for afternoon tea or a special treat; and Savouries for lunch on the go.

But what recipes to stick with and what to change?

We split the list into:

1. The Fitzbillies Classics – the cakes that we would continue making using exactly the same recipes, starting of course with the Chelsea bun.

2. The cakes that we would stop making because we felt they were not of sufficient quality, not to modern tastes or simply not different enough from something else to justify their slot on the cake list.

3. The cakes that we wanted to continue making, but which needed a recipe upgrade to make them the delicious, best version of themselves.

4. New recipes that we loved and felt filled gaps in the repertoire and would be popular.

The list has changed over the past eight years, but usually at the margins. The Classics remain unchallenged: Chelsea buns, scones, Florentines, giant English macaroons, sausage rolls. They were all on the list in 1938, and when we reopened the doors in August 2011 – and they are still on the list now.

New tastes

So, what has changed since 1938 and even since 2011? Tastes in cakes have changed in that time. In 1938, the most popular cutting cake was the special Fitzbillies sponge cake – a fatless sponge. Celebration cakes were mainly made with Genoise sponge. To modern tastes, these cakes would seem very dry and very sweet, so the brief to the bakers nowadays is always: less sweet, more moist.

The newer cakes that are taking over now are influenced by American and Australian baking traditions: sponges made with oil rather than butter and containing fresh fruit or vegetables – visible, grated or as a pureé in the cake (think carrot cake, beetroot in chocolate cake). They are becoming part of the British high-street bakery canon, so we have no shame in including friands (Australian) and red velvet cake (thoroughly American) in a book on British baking.

New needs

Since 2011, the demand for gluten-free food has increased exponentially. We offer lots of cakes that are made 'without gluten-containing ingredients', but of course, because everything is made in a small bakery where wheat flour is in constant use and in the atmosphere, we can never claim that anything is gluten-free.

Most of our non-gluten-containing cakes are made with nuts, particularly ground almonds. Al's favourite cakes are made with ground almonds, and marzipan is a favourite food in our household, so for us that is a better solution (where possible) than gluten-free flour and the chalky texture you so often get with it. Our Sachertorte is very popular for non-gluten-containing birthday cakes, and Florentines, macaroons and clementine and cranberry cake are all made without gluten-containing ingredients.

In the past three years, the most important change in eating habits has been the rapid increase in veganism. We were fortunate that our date slice has always been vegan — it is made using a 'clean label' sunflower margarine. Our bakers have really enjoyed the challenge of developing more vegan recipes. Our rule is always that we want our vegan cakes to be delicious enough that non-vegans will want to eat them too and not notice that they are vegan. Our current favourites are a wonderfully moist chocolate coconut brownie, lemon and blueberry muffin and sticky pear and ginger upside-down cake.

A lot of our original recipes are shamelessly high in fat, sugar and carbohydrates. We'd rather enjoy them in moderation than make them less delicious. As we add new items onto the menu, though, we do look to increase healthier options. To make it onto the Fitzbillies menu today, a new recipe will probably have to tick at least one of the following boxes:

- Vegan
- Made with non-gluten-containing ingredients
- Contains fresh fruit or vegetables
- Less sweet

If you can find recipes that tick all of them and are irresistibly delicious to people who do not eat a restricted diet (as well as to those who do), please let us know.

A day in the life of Fitzbillies

Fitzbillies opens every day of the year except Christmas and New Year's Day. The original cake shop opens at 9am and closes at 6pm as it always has, but now that we have two coffee shops and a separate bakery, there's something happening in some part of the place all day and most of the night…

9pm

The Fitzbillies day starts at 9pm when the night bakers arrive at the bakery, change into their whites and inspect the list for that night's bake. Our wholesale customers plan their orders up till 6pm, so the bakers never know what they will find. Hundreds of dinner rolls for college feasts, brioche buns for burgers in gastropubs and always loaves and loaves of sourdough bread for toast at Fitzbillies. The bakers get started with the weighing out, then mixing and proving, and by 1am, loaves are beginning to come out of the big stone-floored ovens and into the wire cooling baskets.

4am

The last batches are coming out of the ovens and the packers and drivers arrive to get the bread ready for delivery. This is the time to visit the bakery. The wire cooling baskets are filled with every kind of bread, stacked up high. Thousands of loaves and individual rolls. By 7am it will all be gone. The entire production cycle in ten hours, every night.

6am

The cake bakers arrive. Their first job is to roll the Chelsea bun dough, which has been set to prove hours earlier by the night bakers. They roll it super-thin so that it covers an entire table, slather it with brown sugar and currants and roll it up tight. Then it's cut into slices and put into the tins to bake. Once the buns are out of the oven, they are brushed with warm bun syrup and flipped over so that the bottoms can be syrup-ed too. These are the last things to be loaded onto the vans to get to the shops before opening time.

7am

As the vans leave the bakery, laden with breads and baked goods, for the short drive into town, the Fitzbillies chefs are arriving to start breakfast prep and the baristas are switching on coffee machines. They help the drivers unload the vans, wheeling in trolleys laden with trays and trays of Chelsea buns. Time to display these on the counters, just before opening.

8am

Doors open at the coffee shops and the regular morning customers who work nearby come in on their way to the office. Bacon roll in a freshly baked white bap? Homemade granola with yoghurt and fruit compote to eat at your desk later? The bicycle rush hour starts from 8.45 as waves and waves of undergraduates stream past both branches on their way to labs, classes, tutorials and lectures. Don't try to get a coffee at Trumpington Street at 8.55 because the last hopefuls are trying to get their order in before lectures start in the Mill Lane Lecture Rooms.

10am

A more leisurely crowd arrives for a proper breakfast. Visitors to town are looking for the Full Fitzbillies Breakfast. Freelancers leave the distractions of home to get some proper work done over a coffee. Department meetings and coffee mornings. Old friends catching up and new contacts on a first meeting. Coffee is drunk, breakfast is eaten or a mid-morning Chelsea bun is devoured. Ideas are exchanged.

In the kitchen, the chefs are preparing lunch: fat, filled bread rolls made in the bakery that morning, bowls of salad, giant pots of soup.

Meanwhile, back at the bakery, the cake bakers are getting on with trays of gooey brownies and delicious date slices; sponge cake bases are filled and iced; macarons are baked in every colour of the rainbow.

12 noon

Time for lunch. Midday shoppers, visitors, academics meeting colleagues. The cafés fill up to capacity and queues form at the takeaway counters. The chefs are prepped and at their stations, waiting for the tickets to come off the printer. The specials of the day are on the blackboards – today's soup, savoury tart, salads. The regular customers have their favourites: eggs Benedict, chicken and asparagus salad and buck rarebit. And a Full English seems to work at any time of day.

2.30–3.30pm

We call this the lull. If you arrive at either branch of Fitzbillies at this time, you might be mistaken for thinking it was a slow day. But we know it's simply time for us to regroup and wait for the teatime rush.

4pm

Scone o'clock. Magically a queue appears at the door. Well, if you found yourself in Cambridge at 4pm with a few moments or an hour to spare, where would you go? Tea can be anything from an elegant traditional English afternoon tea with a glass of champagne to a brownie in a takeaway bag to eat on the way home.

6pm

Closing time at the branches. Counters cleared and cleaned, chairs up on tables, floor mopped, managers closing checks and everyone's out by 7.30pm. Unbelievable good fortune not to work at night if you're a chef or a waiter.

Back at the bakery, the last of the wholesale orders are coming in and the lists of what's needed for the morning are prepared for the night bakers.

7.30pm–9pm

This is the only time of day when the business isn't working, so we take a deep breath and prepare for it all to start again, as the night bakers leave their homes and make their way to the bakery.

AFTERNOON TEA

Most cultures have grand food rituals, villages roasting whole sheep for a wedding, family Seders, great pasta feasts on tables under the olive trees. We in Britain, however, have only a few — the Sunday lunch, maybe the big breakfast fry-up for the hungover — so perhaps that's why we take such indecent delight in a proper afternoon tea. It's one of the biggest attractions at Fitzbillies and the way the customers' faces light up when the chrome stand is lifted onto their table can ease even the toughest shift. Afternoon tea is a little bit of magic.

We'd always planned to do a proper afternoon tea at Fitzbillies. The bakers could make smaller versions of some of our most popular cakes, the tea could be served in a pot and the special, three-tiered stand would be a breathtaking piece of table theatre, but we were having trouble with the little 'finger' sandwiches. Our first attempts were clumsy and labour-intensive, and then chef Rosie Sykes came to the rescue with a trade secret that fascinated and delighted us all.

There are four sandwiches in an afternoon tea: cucumber, cheese and chutney, ham and mustard and smoked salmon. Two are on brown bread, two on white, and all must be cut to precisely the same size, around 2cm x 8cm. Rosie asked our bread bakers to feed a white and a brown sandwich loaf through the slicer 'end first', creating long horizontal slices. Working with two loaves, one white, one brown, the chef makes one long 'loaf-length' sandwich of the first filling, then another of the next filling on top of that, and so on. By the time she's finished there is one giant multi-deck sandwich made with four slices each of two breads and four different fillings. When the time comes to 'plate up' an afternoon tea, the chef slices off all four sandwiches in a single stroke, all perfectly matched, and lays them out on the stand.

You can pay anything up to £80 for afternoon tea in a London hotel and it's seen as a refined, often feminine treat. That's not our experience at Fitzbillies. There doesn't seem to be anyone who isn't thrilled by a big pile of tiny food. Perhaps the happiest reaction we've seen was from a large Varsity rugby player who came in for a post-match tea with his mum. His smile filled the room.

Baking tips

- In our bakery, the cakes are made on 60cm x 40cm baking trays. The ovens and racks are set up to hold these trays. Batch sizes are set by the size of the trays: 40 Chelsea buns fit on one tray – eight by five. A tray of date slice is cut into 48 bars.

  For the purposes of this book, we have divided the recipe that we would use to make one of our trays by four so that it is the perfect amount for a domestic 30cm square tin.

- The celebration cakes are all scaled down for 18cm-diameter cake tins.

- During and after the war, butter was in short supply and expensive, so home and commercial bakers used margarine. Sometimes that margarine did taste pretty awful (some cakes really do need the taste of butter). Then there was a backlash against margarine. All margarine, in all baking. A good home baker or artisan baker was expected to use unsalted butter in absolutely everything, whether or not it was the best fat for the job. For many years we subscribed to the 'Butter is always Best' school of baking. At the same time, Unilever and other manufacturers put millions of pounds into making better, healthier, more specialised margarines, some of them specifically for baking.

  At Fitzbillies we use butter for some bakes, 'clean label' vegetable margarine for others and corn or sunflower oil for a few more. Whatever is best for that particular recipe. And sometimes we use a mixture if that gives the best result. Butter for shortbread, friands, buttercream icing – wherever the butter flavour is important and it gives a good texture without being greasy. Vegetable margarine where you need a very light, ungreasy texture and to make things vegan, as in our date slice. It also makes great scones. Sunflower or corn oil for carrot cake, red velvet cake and vegan brownies. A mixture of 50/50 butter and margarine for the lightest, tastiest Victoria or lemon sponge and for most of our sweet pastry.

  In the following recipes we say whether we would use butter, margarine or a mixture, based on what we think works best, but if you have strong views, the recipes will still work with any fat.

- Likewise, feel free to grease your tins with butter, lard, margarine or oil spray, or line with a non-stick baking sheet where appropriate, unless otherwise specified.

- Unless otherwise specified, all eggs are medium and butter is unsalted.

Chelsea buns

Though something very much like it probably existed long before, the Chelsea bun entered history as a fashionable indulgence, endorsed by royalty, around 1700. The Chelsea Bun House was one of the many attractions on the approach road to Ranelagh Gardens, playground of Georgian London, and on the day it first began selling them, 'Chelsea' buns took off with the same sort of insane trajectory as modern macarons. According to the 'Curiosities of London', a series of sketches of London life written by John Timbs in 1855 while he was deputy editor of *The Illustrated London News*:

> 'It was customary for the Royal Family and the nobility and gentry to visit the Bun-house in the morning. George II., Queen Caroline, and the princesses frequently honoured the proprietor, Richard Hands, with their company; as did also George III. and Queen Charlotte; her Majesty presented Mrs. Hands with a silver half gallon mug with five guineas in it.'

Though we envy Hands most his nickname of 'Captain Bun', we should perhaps be more impressed with a wife who took her drink by the half gallon. She was clearly an impressive woman who, on her husband's death, continued to run the business with increasing success. It seemed that, much like today, Easter is the peak time for bun-slingers and…

> 'On Good Friday mornings upwards of 50,000 persons have assembled here, when disturbances often arose amongst the London mob; and on one day more than £250 have been taken for buns.'

It must be said that 50,000 people, even allowing some latitude for counting on the day, seems a bit of a stretch. Fitzbillies has never yet had to resort, as Mrs Hands did, to shuttered windows with serving hatches and a large police presence, but we live in hope. Perhaps predictably, though, the run of success was not to last, as Timbs recorded:

> 'The Bun-house was also much frequented by visitors to Ranelagh, after the closing of which, the bun trade declined. Notwithstanding, on Good Friday, April 18, 1839 upwards of 240,000 buns were sold here.'

The Bun House legacy

Later that year the Chelsea Bun House was sold and demolished. The name, however, persisted and Chelsea buns became a popular line in bakeries all over the country, retaining an air of London sophistication and a touch of royal glamour.

In 1855, Anne Manning, a prolific Victorian novelist, published *The Old Chelsea Bun-House*. Her particular style – mildly sensational historical tales written in archaic language and printed in old-style fonts – makes it all but impossible to read now, but it's clear that the original bun-house was still fixed enough in the collective memory to make it worth setting a popular novel amongst its denizens.

Perhaps more than any other traditional bun, the Chelsea is a product of commercial-scale baking. Although there were probably recipes similar to it, it would have been impossible to make a proper Chelsea bun in even the best-equipped home kitchen.

The bakers' way

In a bakery, though, the Chelsea is a comparatively simple thing to create. The standard yeast dough, usually enriched with eggs, is used for a few different kinds of roll or small fancy loaf, so it's easy to embellish it. The dough is rolled out on a long bench, smeared with butter, sprinkled with dried fruit and spices and then rolled tightly into a long sausage.

Then comes the special part… the sausage is sliced into round pieces, a swirl of fruit now enticingly on show, and the slices are packed into a high-sided baking tin and allowed to rise so that they squish into rough squares. Bakers refer to rolls that are cooked touching each other and then torn apart as 'batch'. They're usually cheaper to make than individually baked rolls, which require more oven space. The torn sides might originally have been regarded as a bit of an imperfection of 'factory' cooking. In the Chelsea bun, however, the over-packed oven creates its unique feature.

There's something lovely about that. Something about the cunning of the baker, making something irresistible out of things lying around the bakery, finding ways of adding value and ultimately making it even cheaper to produce.

The Fitzbillies Chelsea bun

In the Fitzbillies kitchen, the enriched dough for the buns is rolled out thinly on 'the sheeter'. This bit of kit looks like it dates from around the 1950s – heavy castings painted cream and lots of chrome. It's basically two canvas conveyor belts with something like an adjustable mangle in between. A big lump of dough is run backwards and forwards through the rollers as the baker gently turns the lever that moves the rollers closer together, much like a pasta maker. There's a modern equivalent called a laminator, but our bakers aren't keen on unnecessary new-fangledness and the sheeter lives on.

Once it's thin enough, the whole sheet of dough is transferred to the long table, which is about 3m of polished stainless steel. The sheet is buttered, the fruit added and everything rolled up tight.

Many of the bakers can handle the Chelseas, but no-one has the amazing talent of head baker Gill for the slicing process. She takes the 'bun knife', an ancient butcher's sabre that's believed to be as old as the bakery, takes a quick glance at the length of the sausage and then cuts it perfectly into exactly the right number to fit the tray. No guides, no measures, no jigs. She never gets it wrong. Even when you've watched it a thousand times, you still won't believe it isn't witchcraft.

Baking the bun

Originally our buns were made in full-size baking trays, 80cm x 45cm in size, and took 60 buns at a time. They were huge, heavy things and it always amazed us to see small bakers slinging the trays into the decks of the hot oven. It took a long time to persuade the bakers, but the one modification we've allowed ourselves in the process is to reduce the size of the tray to make baking slightly less of a heavy workout. The custom-made bun trays we use now are 60cm x 40cm, taking 40 buns arranged eight by five.

The trays of risen buns are put into the oven to bake. In the early days Fitzbillies had a gas-fired oven at the base of a 10m-high brick chimney, but that, sadly, perished in the fire of 1998. Today we use state-of-the art commercial ovens that enable us to control heat from above and below the buns, as well as the humidity in the baking chamber.

There are many recipes for Chelsea buns, old and new, that rest on the richness of the filling and just dress the top with sprinklings of sugar, light coats of icing or a modest sugar-water glaze. This is where the Fitzbillies Chelsea bun made a technical leap forward that, to our minds, mirrors the discovery of the electron, the structure of DNA and the first semi-conductor in the buildings around the bakery. If stickiness was popular, if sugar was good and a glaze was desirable, then how much more thrilling would a secret ingredient be that combined and enhanced them all?

Sticky goodness

Our bun syrup is custom-made for us in a specialist sugar refinery on the outskirts of London. The delicious, old-school dark quality isn't deemed fashionable any more, and though a simple 'golden' syrup might do the job for others, we wanted the authentic taste. Our refiners make syrups for a lot of old craftsman-made products – beers, traditional gingerbreads and the like – and have managed to create something that's extra-sticky, not too cloyingly sweet and with some of the smoky mysterious character of molasses. It must be good… we go through over eight tons of it every year.

THERE ARE 40 BUNS IN A TRAY OF CHELSEAS

Each one is 7.5cm x 7.5cm. The height varies every day because the yeast in the dough responds differently to moisture in the air and atmospheric pressure. Weight also varies because the amount of rise affects how much syrup a bun can absorb. It's an artisanal product, hand-made, and some things can't be entirely controlled.

> On a busy day, we make 20 trays — that's 800 buns.
> In Easter week, we make 100 trays — that's 4,000 buns.
> Last year, we made around 160,000 Chelsea buns.

Gill Abbs joined the business in May 1971, which makes 48 years in service to the bun. She thinks that about seven and half million buns have been made in that time. For most of that time making the Chelseas was her main job. In the past few years she has shared it more and more, so, allowing for holidays and the odd day off, Gill has made over 5 million Chelsea buns.

At 7.5cm per bun, if we could lay those 5 million in a line, it would stretch 375km. Enough to stretch from Cambridge beyond Brussels or, if you prefer, up to the International Space Station.

The unique feature of a Fitzbillies bun has always been the truly spectacular amount of syrup we manage to get into each one, and so it's this final stage, if anything, that would have to be regarded as our 'trade secret'. Once the buns are cooked, we generously brush the tops with warmed syrup. Then the buns are flipped onto another tray, now 'face down' in the syrup, allowing us to syrup their bottoms.

Customers are sometimes puzzled by our strange ritual of serving the buns, because when the trays are placed in the window, the buns are still upside down, sitting waiting in a pool of syrup. The server breaks each bun away from the others with a pair of tongs and kind of swooshes it around in the syrup to pick up every last drop before flipping it over to serve. Which is how your Chelsea bun arrives — the right way up, with a golden-brown crust, flecked with juicy currants and literally 'dripping' with sweetness.

The recipe for Fitzbillies Chelsea buns has always been a closely guarded secret and it remains so to this day. It depends on ingredients like our special bun syrup and equipment not readily available to the home baker. But we do recognise that not everyone is lucky enough to be able to cycle along Trumpington Street every day and stop for an original Fitzbillies Chelsea bun. So, we've developed a Chelsea bun recipe designed for baking in a domestic kitchen that's (almost) as satisfyingly sticky as the original version. Here you are…

Chelsea buns

Makes 16 buns
410g strong white flour, plus extra for dusting
50g caster sugar
½ tsp salt
50g unsalted butter, softened, plus extra
   for greasing
1 medium egg
30g fresh yeast
170ml warm hand-hot water, around 37°C
100g unsalted butter, melted
90g light brown soft sugar
40g white granulated sugar
15g ground cinnamon
210g currants
500g golden syrup

Mix the flour, caster sugar and salt together
in the bowl of a stand mixer. Add the softened
butter and egg and mix with the dough hook.

In a bowl, add the yeast to the warm water and
mix so that it dissolves. Pour the yeast mixture
into the mixer and mix on a slow speed for 3
minutes, then for another 5 minutes on a medium
speed until the dough is smooth and shiny.

Cover with cling film or a damp tea towel
and leave in a warm place for 1 hour, or until
doubled in size.

Grease and line with baking parchment
a 30cm square cake or roasting tin.

Turn the dough out onto a lightly floured surface
and roll out to a 50cm x 36cm rectangle, keeping
the sides straight and the corners square. Make
sure to move the dough occasionally so that it
doesn't stick, but avoid using more flour than
you need on the top of the dough.

Arrange the rectangle of dough so that one of
the long edges is nearest you at the front edge
of the surface. Brush two thirds of the melted
butter onto the dough, right up to the edges.

Mix together the sugars and the cinnamon and
sprinkle this and then the currants evenly over
the dough, leaving a 3cm strip of 'naked' dough
along the edge furthest from you. (It's important
to do this so that the dough seals well when you
roll it up.) Roll the dough up tightly away from
you, like a Swiss roll. Brush the roll all over with
the remaining melted butter.

Cut the roll into 16 slices, each about 3cm wide.
The easiest way is to cut the roll in half, then
each half in half to make quarters, then each
quarter in half to make eighths and then each
of those in half to give you 16 pieces. Don't
worry if the end pieces are a bit messy, as you
can put them messy side down in the tin.

Arrange the buns evenly in four rows of four
with equal spaces between each bun and round
the edge. Place the end buns neat side up.

Cover the buns with cling film or a damp tea towel and leave to prove in a warm place until they are nearly touching each other. This is likely to take between 30 minutes and 1 hour depending on temperature.

While the buns are proving, preheat the oven to 200°C (180°C fan).

When the buns have proved, place the tin in the oven and bake them for 25 minutes until golden brown. During the last 10 minutes of cooking time, warm the syrup in a pan until hot and runny but not boiling.

As soon as the buns are out of the oven, use a large, wide pastry brush to brush a generous amount of syrup all over the buns, right up to the edges. Leave in the baking tin for 10 minutes.

After 10 minutes, turn the buns out onto another baking tray and brush the bottoms (now the tops) all over with syrup. Leave them like this to cool and then cover until ready to serve. They are delicious served warm or cold.

To serve the buns, ease them apart with a knife and turn them over onto a plate.

HEAD BAKER (CAKES): GILL ABBS

Gill is the longest-serving member of the Fitzbillies staff and still the most energetic. She took her City and Guilds in Bakery and Confectionery at Cambridge College of Arts and Technology when she was 19 years old. She served her apprenticeship at the Copper Kettle and Tyler's bakeries, and then joined Fitzbillies under Mr and Mrs Day in 1971. It wasn't a difficult decision because it was, she explains, the 'most prestigious bakery' in the town.

Gill has been a kind of human repository for the collective memory of the bakery. Until recently, when recipes began to be recorded for the tracking of allergens, our whole repertoire of cakes resided in Gill's brain and a small collection of well-worn index cards. This is not to say that she's secretive or protective about her methods; in her years with us she's done amazing work in improving and updating, in adapting new recipes and always quietly guiding generations of new young bakers.

It's easy to imagine that working in a bakery is a delicate process of coaxing lightness out of doughs and the precise and delicate application of decorations, but Gill knows the truth. A bakery is like any workshop or small factory, with long hours, heavy lifting and the constant wrangling of complicated machinery. Gill hasn't just had the strength to succeed at this, but also an incredible flexibility in embracing new ideas. When one of the old ovens was retired and replaced with a modern computerised version, we all feared Gill would be resistant to the change. Within a couple of days, she'd not only tested and adapted most of her recipes to the new oven, she'd programmed it to play a tune when it finished cooking.

Gill remains at the heart of what is now a modern, state-of-the-art bakery, but she still has one very old-fashioned idea that she refuses to let go of. When we asked her why she'd come back to Fitzbillies and stayed with us when she was so obviously pursued by other companies, she said, simply, 'It's my job. You've got to stay to keep up standards', and went back to shaping buns.

SCONES & MORNING GOODS

There's no experience quite as overwhelming for a food lover as driving a van full of hot baked goods through empty streets as the sun comes up — you'll never forget that smell.

You can buy cakes in a supermarket if you're so inclined, but what distinguishes a really good bakery are the trays of fresh stuff coming hot from the ovens every morning. There is nothing to beat a cake or pastry still warm from the oven with no preservatives or special packaging and a 'shelf life' that's measured in a few joyful hours rather than miserable, plastic-wrapped weeks. If you're lucky, the muffin you have with your coffee was still a pile of raw ingredients when you went to bed last night.

Nothing better expresses the workings of a bakery than the things that are made fresh, every night, carefully packed and brought across town to serve to you at the absolute peak of deliciousness. But with these recipes, the home baker has for once the advantage over the professionals. You only have to 'deliver' these from your oven to the plate.

English muffins

At Fitzbillies we make and serve hundreds of English muffins each week. They are usually hidden underneath eggs Benedict, eggs Florentine or eggs Royale and are the unsung heroes of some of the most popular dishes on our brunch menu. They are equally good toasted and served with butter for tea on a winter afternoon.

Makes 12 muffins
190ml milk, full-fat or semi-skimmed, cold
190ml warm hand-hot water, around 37°C
40g unsalted butter, softened, plus extra for
    greasing, or use cooking oil
305g plain flour
305g strong white flour, plus extra for dusting
16g salt
8g caster sugar
12g fresh yeast
7g dried active yeast
250g semolina, for dusting the baking tray

Using a stand mixer with a dough hook, put the milk, warm water and butter into the mixing bowl, then add the flours, salt, sugar and yeasts, making sure the yeasts and the salt are kept as far away from each other as possible (as the salt will attack and weaken the yeast). Mix on a slow setting for about 4 minutes, scraping down the sides of the bowl occasionally, then turn the mixer onto a faster setting for approximately 4 minutes, or until the dough looks smooth and shiny. The dough should be fairly wet, so try to resist adding extra flour, as this is the secret to amazing pillow-soft muffins.

Tip out onto a lightly floured surface, knead gently for 30 seconds and then return the dough to the bowl. The dough will feel slightly warm; don't worry, this is all part of the process to encourage the yeast activity. Cover the bowl with a damp tea towel, cling film or a large plate. Leave at room temperature for an hour, during which it will increase in volume.

Now turn the dough out onto a lightly floured work surface and divide into 12 pieces, about 90g each. Shape them in your hands into round balls – don't worry if your balls are misshapen, as they will come out fine in the end.

Dust a baking tray with semolina and arrange the dough balls on it. Cover with a damp tea towel and leave at room temperature for 30 minutes.

Warm a griddle pan, flat grill or heavy-bottomed pan on a medium heat on the hob. You will be using metal muffin rings, so please don't use your best non-stick pan. Grease your muffin rings with butter or cooking oil and place them onto the hot pan — the rings work best when they are hot. When your dough balls are ready, gently drop them into the rings on the hot pan. After 7 minutes, remove the rings, leaving the muffins on the pan.

Turn the muffins over (the tops should be a nice golden colour) and leave on the pan for a further 7 minutes, then remove and place on a cooling rack. You will need to do this in batches. Allow to cool, then slice, toast and slather with butter.

Fruit scones

Whenever anyone asks Alison what her favourite cake is, she replies, 'Well, it's not really a cake, but scone, jam and cream.' After the Chelsea bun, it's the sweet item we sell most of in the café. Cream tea is surely one of English cookery's greatest gifts to the world.

Makes 10 large or 14 small scones
460g plain flour, plus extra for dusting
30g baking powder
50g caster sugar
80g unsalted butter, cold and cubed
2 medium eggs
200ml milk, full-fat or semi-skimmed
120g sultanas

Preheat the oven to 190°C (170°C fan) and line a baking sheet with baking parchment.

Mix together the flour, baking powder and caster sugar in a large bowl. Rub in the butter with your fingertips.

Lightly beat together the eggs and milk in a separate bowl. Reserve a tablespoon of the milk and egg mix to glaze the top of the scones.

Add the liquid to the dry mix and bring together with your hands. Stir in the sultanas last so that they don't get broken up.

Turn the mixture out onto a lightly floured work surface and give it the very lightest of kneads — just two folds should do — to make sure it comes together evenly. Roll out to 3cm thick and cut out to the size you want. We use a 7cm cutter for large scones and a 5cm cutter for smaller scones.

Place the scones spaced well apart on the lined baking sheet and brush with the reserved beaten milk and egg. Bake the large scones for 15–20 minutes and the smaller scones for 12–15 minutes until they are lightly golden.

Serve either warm or cold, with jam and clotted cream, obviously.

Cheese scones

Cheese scones work any time of day. They're not too indulgent for breakfast, they make a hearty mid-morning snack, go well with soup in the café at lunchtime or satisfy those who prefer a savoury treat at tea time. And if we are catering for a drinks party, we make lots of tiny cheese scones as canapé bases – they are fantastic with a herby cream cheese topping.

Makes 10 large or 14 small scones
400g plain flour, plus extra for dusting
60g wholemeal flour
30g baking powder
85g unsalted butter, cold and cubed
1 medium egg, lightly beaten
10g chives, chopped
30g wholegrain mustard
200g strong Cheddar cheese, grated,
    plus extra for topping
300ml milk, full-fat or semi-skimmed,
    plus extra for brushing the tops of
    the scones

Preheat the oven to 190°C (170°C fan) and line a baking sheet with baking parchment.

Mix together the flours and baking powder in a large bowl. Then rub in the butter with your fingertips.

Add the egg, chives, wholegrain mustard and cheese and stir through. Add the milk and bring everything together with your hands.

Turn the mixture onto a floured work surface and give it the lightest of kneads – just two folds should do – to make sure it comes together evenly. Roll out to 3cm thick and cut out to the size you want. We use a 7cm cutter for large scones and a 5cm cutter for smaller scones.

Place the scones well apart on the baking sheet. Brush the tops with milk and put a little clump of grated cheese in the middle of each. Bake for 15–20 minutes for large scones or 12–15 minutes for the smaller ones until they are lightly golden.

Serve warm with salted butter.

Lemon & blueberry vegan muffins

When we develop recipes for vegan or gluten-free cakes, we always want to make them so delicious that someone who is not vegan or gluten-intolerant will want to eat them too. These muffins are light, fruity and pretty irresistible. You can also bake this recipe as a loaf or round cake – which we often do for vegan birthdays.

Makes 12 muffins
For the crumble topping
25g vegan margarine
40g plain flour
40g light brown soft sugar

For the muffin mix
420g self-raising flour
190g caster sugar
¾ tsp baking powder
¾ tsp bicarbonate of soda
370ml soya milk
240ml sunflower oil
zest and juice of 2 lemons
200g fresh blueberries

Preheat the oven to 180°C (160°C fan) and place paper muffin cases in a 12-hole muffin tin.

First make the crumble topping by rubbing the margarine into the flour and sugar in a bowl. Put to one side.

Mix together the flour, sugar, baking powder and bicarbonate of soda in a large bowl.

Mix together the soya milk, sunflower oil and lemon zest and juice in another bowl, then pour this into the dry ingredients. Stir until just combined.

Fold in 125g of the blueberries, saving the remaining 75g so that you have two or three blueberries for the top of each muffin.

Spoon the mixture evenly into the 12 muffin cases. Put two or three blueberries on the top of each and then sprinkle the crumble mixture over the top. Bake for 35–40 minutes until the muffins spring back to the touch. Remove from the oven and leave to cool in the tin.

Banana muffins

Like many of our newer recipes, these muffins are influenced by American baking and that most wonderful of 1950s American bakers, Maida Heatter (search out her books and bake all her recipes!). These muffins, adapted from one of her recipes, are deliciously moist and fly off our coffee-shop counters at breakfast time. You can also bake the recipe as a banana loaf or iced cake.

Makes 12 muffins
130g unsalted butter, softened
310g caster sugar
½ tsp vanilla extract
2 ripe or overripe bananas
¾ tsp bicarbonate of soda
2 medium eggs
130g walnuts, chopped
310g plain flour
1 ½ tsp baking powder
½ tsp salt
120ml buttermilk
40g coconut chips
40g banana chips

Preheat the oven to 180°C (160°C fan) and place paper muffin cases in a 12-hole muffin tin.

Cream the butter, sugar and vanilla extract in a bowl until pale and creamy.

Peel and mash the bananas in a separate bowl with the bicarbonate of soda. Put to one side. It will fizz a little.

Add the eggs to the butter and sugar mix, one at a time, stirring after each addition. Then add the banana, followed by the walnuts, and mix to combine. Add the flour, baking powder and salt and mix until just combined.

Add the buttermilk and mix again until just combined (do not overmix or you will make tough muffins). Spoon the mixture evenly into the 12 muffin cases and top with coconut and banana chips. Bake for 25–30 minutes until the tops spring back when touched. Remove from the oven and leave to cool in the tin.

Savoury courgette muffins

The grated courgette in these muffins keeps them
wonderfully moist, like the carrot in a carrot
cake. The feta, sun-dried tomatoes and Parmesan
add an irresistible salty, savoury, umami taste.
Great for a savoury breakfast or picnic.

Makes 12 muffins
200g plain flour
40g jumbo oats
2 tsp baking powder
½ tsp bicarbonate of soda
1 tsp salt
½ tsp black pepper
8g basil leaves, chopped
60g Parmesan, grated
2 medium eggs
250ml buttermilk
4 tbsp olive oil
200g courgette, grated
40g pine nuts

For the topping
40g sun-dried tomatoes,
    chopped into small pieces
40g feta cheese, chopped into cubes
20g Parmesan, grated

Preheat the oven to 230°C (210°C fan) and place
paper muffin cases in a 12-hole muffin tin.

Mix together the flour, oats, baking powder,
bicarbonate of soda, salt, pepper, basil and
Parmesan in a bowl.

In a separate bowl, beat together the eggs,
buttermilk and oil. Pour the wet ingredients over
the dry ingredients. Stir to combine, then add
the grated courgette and pine nuts and stir until
just combined (do not overmix or you will make
tough muffins).

Spoon the mixture evenly into the 12 muffin
cases. Top with the pieces of sun-dried tomato
and feta and sprinkle over the Parmesan. Bake
for 20–25 minutes until the muffin tops have
domed and they spring back to the touch.
Remove from the oven and leave to cool in the tin.

THE BOSS: ALISON WRIGHT

They say that the success of a business depends on understanding its customers, and that's not difficult for Alison – she's been one for as long as she can remember. For her 21st birthday, Al had a *croquembouche* from Fitzbillies, made – as we established later – by current head baker Gill Abbs. She used to cycle past the shop on her way home from school, dropping in on occasions to pick up a fondant fancy or an éclair. When she was even younger, her father, then bursar of St Catharine's College, used to bring home boxes of Chelsea buns... as well he might, because James Wright had acquired the taste for them as an undergraduate and oarsman at Cambridge in the 1960s. Al's maternal grandmother, a redoubtable Cambridge lady, made one exception to her rule against pre-prepared foods in the house – for the Fitzbillies sausage roll.

Her other qualification is that she knows and loves cake. With Al, the usual childhood love of icing cookies and making flat sponge cakes didn't stop there. While she worked in marketing, she'd spend her holidays and weekends attending baking and cake-decorating courses. She'd make a five-tier wedding cake for a friend's wedding and blow them out of the water at the office Bake Off or school cake sale. All she needed was an outlet for her baking. She's not the only person to have dreamed of owning a cake shop – but not everyone actually acts on that dream.

It was Al who responded instinctively and leaped into action when she learned that Fitzbillies had gone bankrupt, and she's the driving force behind its success today. She combines a fierce love for, and pride in, the business with a ruthless, analytical approach to its management and constant improvement. You might think a degree in PPE (Philosophy, Politics and Economics) from *the other place* and a 20-year career in marketing and advertising was overqualification for running a provincial cake shop – but she would absolutely disagree. She'd say she uses all those skills every day to help make Fitzbillies better: better for customers, better cakes, brunch, coffee; better able to survive and thrive when other high-street bakery businesses have gone to the wall. She'd also say she couldn't do any of it without Tim and the team of 60 brilliant people who work at Fitzbillies.

If you can keep her still for long enough, ask her her favourite question: 'How come Fitzbillies is doing so well now when it was bankrupt eight years ago?' She'll tell you. In some detail.

FANCY CAKES

There is something so lovely about the word 'fancy'; it's so weirdly British.

It doesn't overclaim like 'premium' or belittle anyone else like 'superior'. It's part of the peculiar lexicon of traditional high-street businesses. We still see 'fancy' written on many of the ingredients we buy, like a sack of sugar or a tub of syrup; it means a 'better than ordinary' grade. Higher quality but stopping short of anything as extravagant as 'luxury'.

And this is precisely where 'fancy cakes' fit into the Fitzbillies repertoire. They were a little bit exotic, but not confusingly foreign. They were a little bit indulgent, though not in a way that would make people at the next table throw disapproving glances. They were out of the ordinary without being odd – a little adventure that no-one could possibly want to deny themselves. Delicious in a reassuringly modest way.

We have an incredibly soft spot for our fancy cakes because they represent so accurately the original ethos of Fitzbillies. Most have been on the menu since the shop was founded and we've tried hard to stay as close to the original recipes as we can. Already these lovely old cakes have a retro feeling to them and there's certainly competition from exciting new recipes and trends with every passing month. But no matter how tastes change, Fitzbillies will have fancy cakes on the counter forever.

British 'Fancy Cakes'

For the longest time, a bakery was a fixture on the British high street like a butcher or candlestick maker or any other of the Happy Families pack. The British high-street baker is also appreciably different from those you'll find in any other country, unique to us and the culmination of a very specific series of historical and cultural influences.

During the Industrial Revolution, the majority of the population of the UK drifted towards towns and cities. Here, separated from the traditional infrastructure of local wheat farms, flour mills and home baking, they were fed through a new network – industrial bulk milling and bread manufactured in local bakeries. These were effectively small factories where workers used machines to mix and shape dough. For the first time, they could bake a consistent commercial product in larger batches that could be priced and sold against increasing local competition. It was a huge leap in a short period of time from the village bakehouse that had remained unchanged for centuries, and it was cutting-edge stuff, becoming an essential link in feeding an urbanising society.

The advent of sugar

The complicated and difficult history of sugar in the British diet has been extensively covered elsewhere, but it is fair to say that by the time of the Industrial Revolution, we had a powerful addiction to the stuff that ranged across all classes and regions. The Brits liked sweet things, they saw them as simple pleasures and indulgences and also perhaps as affordable or aspirational luxuries. Bakeries were able to turn their hands to cake and many of our traditional recipes could be produced in larger quantities as affordable treats. Simple buns, sweetened breads and uncomplicated biscuits were already favourites, but with the luxury of the increasing availability of sugar, it was often bakers from countries with more developed sweet baking and confectionery traditions who brought them to the British public.

Great houses had, for many years, favoured French chefs and as a result understood the wider potential of French pastry work, but to ordinary people, such luxurious novelties must have been thrilling. The first bakeries selling 'patisserie' in British cities must have gained quick competitive advantage. The Austrians also had a strong baking game and it wasn't long before the 'Viennoiserie' techniques of layering butter with pastry were also tempting British city dwellers.

By the outbreak of the First World War, a large number of high-street cake shops were under Austrian or German ownership. As war was declared, and particularly later in May 1915 when the *Lusitania* was torpedoed, there was widespread civil unrest in British cities, angry riots that targeted businesses owned by 'enemy' Germans, Austrians or Hungarians. According to the collection of newspaper reports held in the National Archive, 'businesses were targeted on the basis of German-sounding names and, as a trade associated with Germans, bakers were also particularly targeted'.

As a result of the riots – the largest the UK had seen in the 20th century – the government ramped up their policy of deportation and internment, and so by the end of hostilities, the majority of German, Austrian and Hungarian businesses had simply disappeared. The trades that effectively evaporated were an odd selection, but ones that left strange holes in British society. Most specialist 'pork butchers' were Hungarian or Austrian, most of the large sugar refineries were German-owned and staffed, the 'oompah'-style dance bands that toured pubs and dancehalls and supplied the British working class with one of its most widespread entertainments were German and the high-class cake shops, dominated by all three nationalities, were decimated.

The British tradition

In 1894, J. Lyons & Co. launched the first of their Tea Shops, followed by their Corner Houses in 1909. There had been tea rooms for almost as long as we'd had tea, but the Lyons Corner Houses and Tea Shops, with their Art Nouveau styling and aproned 'nippie' waitresses, were something different and fresh. Tea had begun as a luxury for the wealthy and tea rooms had reflected that ethos, but through the Industrial Revolution and as a result of the economic importance of tea consumption to the expanding Empire, the working class acquired a strong taste for it too. By the turn of the century, tea drinking transcended class, a fact that Lyons were the first to acknowledge.

It was said that 'anyone' could walk into a Lyons Tea Shop and feel comfortable. This may not have been entirely true, but it certainly created a vast new market when it became a place where women felt they could dine unaccompanied by men – a huge social breakthrough.

Lyons also owned their own production bakeries for biscuits and cakes and, over time, evolved a repertoire that reflected the democratic nature of their audience. Unpretentious but delicious, luxurious yet unshowy… the roots of a new canon of British bakery.

An entrepreneurial opportunity

The Mason brothers who founded Fitzbillies must have been like any other of the hundreds of thousands of servicemen who returned from the awfulness of war to a much-changed home. It's almost impossible for us to imagine today the mindset of people who'd seen such horror, returning to the place they'd risked everything to defend and having to forge an entirely new life.

It was, though, a time of unparalleled opportunity. Returning servicemen were given a 'demob' payment. A small amount, but perhaps enough to kickstart a new venture. The home market was wide open to them, with thousands of businesses having closed due to the absence or death of their owners. At the same time, reunited families were looking forward to re-establishing a new kind of normality. It has always been true that food businesses are a great entry point for the entrepreneurial. The initial costs are quite low, skills easy to acquire and dedication and hard work – 'sweat equity' as we call it today – can yield fast rewards. In 1918, the bakery business had benefitted from technological advances and was being aggressively touted as an opportunity by equipment manufacturers and ingredients suppliers.

The Mason brothers already had some experience in baking inherited from their father and so would have been able to acquire premises quickly, equipment and ingredients on favourable terms and offer solid jobs to other returning soldiers.

The first years that Fitzbillies traded were the most formative for urban bakers. There was enough residual xenophobia that Viennoiserie or pâtisserie could no longer be the popular model and so a new kind of menu evolved – a combination of British favourites that go back centuries, together with some renamed exotic imports, some quirky innovations and some outright bonkers-ness. It was also marked by that post-war sense of 'democracy'. Cakes began to lose the clear class distinctions of puffs of cream for the posh and punishing little dry cakes for the poor. The new fare tapped into that sense of 'a treat for everyone' and developed into a hugely characteristic repertoire unique to the post-war high street: 'British Fancy Cakes'.

A university appetite

The development of bakeries was a nationwide phenomenon, but there were some conditions, historical and social, that were unique to Cambridge. Universities run on cake. Oh sure, they have 700-year-old dining halls and huge kitchen brigades, but very few of the students or fellows would have had every meal inside the college. Today, student rooms have shared kitchens and microwaves, and many of the porters' lodges have reluctantly learned to handle Deliveroo, but this is really only a decade-old phenomenon. Before the food renaissance hit the city, anyone wanting to eat something that wasn't brought to a 100-foot-long oak table by a college servant had to go to a pub for a pie or sandwich or to a bakery for a bun.

This symbiosis with the University made it possible for Fitzbillies to cling on while in other towns attention was slowly drawn away from cake shops by other attractions. Where a weekly treat for the family might have been a bag of cakes, picked up by Dad on his way home from work on a Friday, he'd now be just as likely to get home and suggest a takeaway. The students remained good customers, always keen for a post-lecture treat, but the days when the cakes were a fixture on the high street were passing.

Chocolate éclairs & coffee choux buns

Éclairs are French patisserie, but they've been part of the English cake-shop canon for so long now that we have almost forgotten their sophisticated origins. They are cream cakes and are therefore 'naughty but nice' and slightly redolent of pantomime or a Carry On film.

*   The coffee choux bun is just a different-shaped éclair with even more comedy potential. If Billy Bunter ever came to Fitzbillies, we like to think that's what he would have chosen.*

Makes 10 éclairs, 20 profiteroles
   or 6 gigantic choux buns
95g unsalted butter
140ml water
130g strong white flour
4 medium eggs
284ml whipping cream

For the chocolate fondant icing
50g 54% dark chocolate
2 tbsp water
150g fondant icing sugar

For the coffee fondant icing
50ml strong coffee
400g fondant icing sugar

Preheat the oven to 190°C (170°C fan) and line two baking sheets with baking parchment.

Put the butter and water into a thick-bottomed pan and bring to the boil.

Stir in the flour and cook over a low heat, beating continuously with a wooden spoon for about 4 minutes until the mixture comes away cleanly from the sides of the pan.

Put the mixture into the bowl of a stand mixer and beat for about a minute until cool. Add the eggs and mix on a high speed for about 3 minutes until the mixture is fully combined and glossy.

Put the mixture into a piping bag and cut off the end to leave an opening about 2cm across. (Or use a plastic freezer bag with the corner cut off.)

For éclairs, pipe 10cm lines of mixture onto the lined baking tray at least 6cm apart to allow for rise. For choux buns, pipe a 'blob' – a small, golf-ball-sized blob for profiteroles, or a tennis-ball sized-blob for choux buns. Again, leave plenty of space between them.

Before you put the piped choux in the oven, spray them with a fine mist of water so that steam is created as they bake.

RECIPE CONTINUED OVERLEAF

Bake the éclairs for 30 minutes, profiteroles for 20 minutes and the choux buns for 35 minutes until puffed up and a light golden colour. Do not open the oven door during the first 25 minutes of cooking or the choux will collapse.

Leave to cool on the tray. (You can freeze the choux at this point, then take them out of the freezer to fill when you are ready to use them.)

Whip the cream until it is quite firm and makes stiff peaks. Put it in a piping bag fitted with a medium-sized, star-shaped nozzle. (Or use a plastic freezer bag with the corner cut off.)

Cut the éclairs, profiteroles or choux buns halfway through horizontally with a serrated knife, leaving one edge attached. While holding them open, pipe in the cream.

To make the chocolate fondant icing, melt the dark chocolate and water together very gently in a pan, stirring continuously. Remove from the heat and add the icing sugar. Stir well until smooth and glossy.

Spread the chocolate icing along the top of the éclairs using a palette knife, or pile the profiteroles on a serving plate and drizzle the icing all over them. Leave to set.

Alternatively, if you are making the coffee choux buns, mix together the strong coffee and icing sugar and ice the top of each bun using a palette knife. Leave to set.

Japonaise cakes

These delightful little cakes are one of the most 'patisserie' things that we make. They do require a bit of time and skill (or at least manual dexterity), but they are thoroughly worth it. They seem to us to come from a different time, when ladies wore tea dresses and ate cakes with tiny forks. If you would like to retreat to that time for a special tea party, these are the cakes for you.

Makes 12 cakes
3 medium egg whites
145g caster sugar
85g ground almonds

For the praline icing
60g caster sugar
25ml water
40g whole blanched hazelnuts
*½ batch of Italian meringue buttercream
   (see recipe on page 117)*

120g roasted, sliced hazelnuts, to decorate

Preheat the oven to 180°C (160°C fan) and line two baking trays with baking parchment.

In the bowl of a stand mixer, whisk together the egg whites and 85g of the caster sugar until the mixture is glossy and forms soft peaks.

In a separate bowl, mix together the ground almonds and the remaining caster sugar. Gently fold the dry ingredients into the egg white mixture, being careful not to knock the air out.

Put the mixture into a piping bag and cut off the end about 1.5cm across. (Or use a plastic freezer bag with the corner cut off.) Pipe 24 evenly sized circles in 5cm diameter, 12 on each baking sheet – they shouldn't spread much (unless they are overmixed). If you are concerned about your ability to pipe even circles, you could use a macaron piping mat or just draw circles on your baking parchment. We pipe blobs rather than piping spirals, but either works.

Bake for 20 minutes until very lightly coloured. Leave to cool completely.

Now make the praline. Dissolve the sugar in the water in a saucepan over a low heat. Add the whole blanched hazelnuts to the sugar syrup and boil for about 4 minutes until the syrup turns deep gold in colour. Do not stir. Remove the saucepan from the heat and quickly and carefully pour the syrup onto a baking sheet lined with baking parchment and leave to cool.

RECIPE CONTINUED OVERLEAF

Once the praline is cool, break it into pieces
and then put into a food processor, reserving
a few nutty shards for decoration. Pulse to a
crunchy powder.

Make the Italian meringue buttercream
according to the recipe on page 117, then gently
fold the praline powder into the meringue. You
are now ready to assemble your Japonaise cakes.

Start by sandwiching pairs of the Japonaise
cakes together with the buttercream, facing the
pointy tops together in the middle so that you
have a flat top and bottom.

Scatter the roasted, sliced hazelnuts on a plate.

Use a palette knife to spread buttercream around
the sides of each 'sandwich' – it doesn't need to
be too perfect – then roll them in the hazelnuts
to cover the sides.

Place each cake in a paper case and pipe or
spread some buttercream on the top. Finish by
placing a nutty shard on top of each cake.

English macaroons

There is no real risk of confusing these macaroons with French macarons. They are made with the same ingredients, but are about ten times the size, chewier and have no truck with pretty pastel colours and fillings. They revel in their simplicity – three ingredients, no decoration and incredibly easy to make. If you're an almond fan, they are absolutely irresistible. We do make and sell French macarons by the thousand, but we think we'll leave those recipes to the experts at Pierre Hermé and Ladurée.

Makes 6 large, 12 small or
18 mini macaroons
150g ground almonds
200g caster sugar
2 large egg whites

Preheat the oven to 170°C (150°C fan) and line a baking tray with baking parchment. Traditionally macaroons were made on edible rice paper, which was left attached to the bottom, but baking parchment or a non-stick baking sheet is easier.

Mix together the ground almonds, caster sugar and egg whites in a bowl with a wooden spoon (it really isn't worth getting the mixer dirty for this one). You should achieve a dropping consistency, firm enough to hold its shape, but soft enough to pipe.

Put the mixture into a piping bag and cut off the end about 2cm across. (Or use a plastic freezer bag with the corner cut off.) Pipe the mixture into 6 large mounds, 12 smaller ones or 18 mini ones, with space between each to allow the mixture to spread. (If you are making 12 or 18, you may need two baking trays.)

Place the tray in the oven and bake until light golden in colour: 15–20 minutes for large macaroons, 10–15 for the smaller ones and 8–10 minutes for the mini ones.

Remove from the oven and leave to cool completely on the tray. They cling quite hard to the baking parchment, so peel them away gently without tearing. If you are using rice paper, you can leave that on the bottom of the macaroons and just tear away the excess round the edge.

Florentines

Florentines have been on the cake list at Fitzbillies from day one. They are one of the cakes that people obsess about and we have customers who come every Friday for a Florentine as an afternoon treat, so it feels like a disaster if we run out. Florentines, by nature, don't contain gluten — just another reason to love them.

Makes 12 large Florentines (or 24 mini ones)
25g honey
55g unsalted butter, plus extra for greasing
40ml water
100g caster sugar
55g glacé cherries
240g flaked almonds
55g flaked hazelnuts
150g 54% dark chocolate

Preheat the oven to 185°C (165°C fan). Grease and line a 30cm x 20cm traybake tin.

Heat the honey, butter and water in a pan until the butter has melted. Add the sugar to the pan and bring to the boil, then remove from the heat.

Roughly chop the cherries and mix together in a bowl with the flaked almonds and hazelnuts.

Pour the honey, butter and sugar mixture over the nuts and cherries and stir gently so as not to break up the nuts.

Tip the mixture into the tin and press it out flat with the palm of your hand until even and filling the tin. Bake for 30–35 minutes until golden, then remove from the oven and leave to cool.

Cut the Florentines into a shape of your choice. We use a circle cutter, or cut them into diamonds to save on wastage. You will get around 12 large Florentines or 24 mini ones.

Melt the chocolate in the microwave (give it 20 seconds on medium and stir, then another 20 seconds until melted), or in a heatproof bowl set over a pan of barely simmering water. Your objective is to keep the temperature at 34°C or below so that the chocolate stays tempered and you get a nice shiny finish.

Spread the chocolate onto the reverse side of each Florentine using a palette knife and leave to set at room temperature, chocolate side up.

Fondant fancies

You've got to love a fondant fancy. Surely the campest of cakes, its very name sounds like "a Kenneth Williams' innuendo". The pastel perfection, on the other hand, seems to date from another time. They look almost too pretty to eat, but eat them you must – a homemade fondant fancy is a truly wonderful thing. They are a little tricky to make, but the key thing is to leave enough time: make the cake and set it up the day before. And practice makes perfect.

Makes 24–30 cakes
1 batch of lemon cake sponge
  (see recipe on page 102)
Italian meringue buttercream
  (see recipe on page 117)
juice of 3 lemons, plus a splash of water
  if needed
1kg fondant icing sugar
a variety of food colouring – anything will
  work – to give you the colour range you
  want (pale pink is our favourite)
Butter, baking margarine or oil spray,
  for greasing
piped decorations for the tops of the cakes,
  e.g. single flowers

Preheat the oven to 180°C (160°C fan) and grease and line a 30cm x 23cm x 5cm rectangular tin. (Any square or rectangular cake tin of about this size is fine.)

Make the lemon cake sponge mixture according the recipe on page 102. Spread the mixture into your tin and bake for 25–30 minutes until it springs back to the touch. Leave to cool completely.

Meanwhile, make the Italian meringue buttercream according to the recipe on page 117. Flavour the buttercream with half the lemon juice (no zest, as it won't spread smoothly).

Remove the cake from the tin and trim the top a little if it is domed. Turn the cake over so that the bottom is now the top – it's very important to have a flat top.

Slice the cake horizontally into two even layers. Spread the bottom layer with a thin coat of Italian meringue buttercream and place the top layer back on top. Spread the top with another thin layer of Italian meringue buttercream. Refrigerate for 30 minutes, or until firm.

Now get a long ruler out. You need to cut the cake into even 4cm squares. Trim off the rough outer edges with a sharp serrated knife first, then use the ruler and a small sharp knife to mark the top of the cake very carefully.

RECIPE CONTINUED OVERLEAF

Once you are happy, cut the cake into the marked squares, making sure to cut straight down vertically through the cake. Refrigerate for another 30 minutes.

Now make the fondant icing – combine the icing sugar with the remaining lemon juice (plus a splash of water if needed), following the instructions on the packet and mixing until smooth and glossy. Divide between two bowls. Leave one bowl of icing white and colour the other bowl of icing whatever colour you wish.

You are now ready to dip your fondants. Carefully pick up a cube of cake at the bottom between your thumb and forefinger. Dip it two thirds of the way into the bowl of fondant, then pull it out and turn it back the right way up so that the fondant drips down to cover the remaining third. Place on a cooling rack to dry.

Keep going until you have dipped all the fondants. It is a tricky, fiddly business. You will end up very sticky… and perhaps a bit irritable, but you will get better at it over time.

Leave all the fondant fancies to set completely. When they are dry, decorate the top as you wish. A single piped flower decoration is traditional. Or for christenings we often pipe the baby's initial. We then like to arrange the fondants on a square plate or board in a chequerboard pattern.

Truffle mice

*Every bakery has recipes designed to use up
leftover cake. Cake truffles are one of these. They
are super-delicious and addictive. We have a
grown-up version – the rum truffle (page 95) –
and a kid's version, the truffle mouse, which is
much cuter. So many Cambridge children have
come to love these for their afternoon treat that
we now make a truffle mouse birthday cake with
baby mice on it. At home there are two options
for making these:*

*1. If you have a leftover chocolate cake that is
getting a bit dry, perhaps a birthday cake that
was too large to finish, this is your opportunity
for making truffle mice.*

*2. Next time you are baking a chocolate cake,
double the recipe and put the extra sponge in the
freezer for when the truffle moment strikes you.*

*Or, of course, you can just start from scratch
and make a chocolate cake.*

> Makes 12 mice
> *For the chocolate cake truffle mix*
> *670g leftover chocolate cake*
>   *(see page 107 for chocolate cake recipe)*
> *55g unsalted butter, softened*
> *135g icing sugar*
> *30g cocoa powder, plus a little extra if needed*
> *1 tbsp milk, plus a little extra if needed*
> *80g raspberry jam*

To finish and decorate the mice
200g milk chocolate
160g 54% dark chocolate
12 currants, to make the noses
24 blanched almonds, to make the ears
1 tube of white icing
1 tube of chocolate icing

Put the chocolate cake (it doesn't matter if it's
got icing on it) in the bowl of a stand mixer
and, using the beater attachment, mix slowly
to break it down into crumbs. Tip into another
bowl and put to one side.

Put the butter, icing sugar, cocoa powder and
milk in the (clean) bowl of the mixer and beat
until smooth and light. Start slowly, with a tea
towel over the mixer so that the kitchen doesn't
get covered in icing sugar, then turn it up to a
fast speed.

Add the jam and cake crumbs to the mixture
and beat on a slow speed to combine into a firm
paste. If the mixture seems too firm to roll into
balls, add a splash of milk. If it seems too soft to
hold its shape, add a little more cocoa powder.

Divide the mixture into 12 equal pieces (you
can weigh them if you are worried about getting
them even, or just go for a mouse family where
some of the members are bigger than others).
Split some of the pieces in two if you want to
make baby mice.

RECIPE CONTINUED OVERLEAF

Roll the pieces into balls, then roll the ball to a slight point at one end (for the mouse's nose) and flatten its bottom a little by pushing the other end in a bit. Place the mice about 2cm apart on a clean cooling rack that is sitting over a baking tray lined with baking parchment.

Melt both chocolates together in one bowl very gently in the microwave (give it 20 seconds on medium and stir, then another 20 seconds until melted), or in a heatproof bowl set over a pan of barely simmering water. The aim is to just melt the chocolate, but not allow it to get hotter than 34°C so that it will stay tempered and set firm and shiny.

Use a small ladle to spoon the chocolate over the mice, trying to achieve good, even coverage, particularly around the head end. The excess chocolate will run off onto the baking parchment in the tray underneath and can be tipped back into the melted chocolate or slightly re-melted if needed to coat the last few mice. Coat the mice in batches, three at a time, as you need to get some decorating done before the chocolate sets.

Take your first three chocolate mice and stick a currant onto the nose of each. As the chocolate sets it will be held in place. Take two blanched almonds and stick them in about a third of the way back from the nose on each mouse, pointed end down, to make rounded mouse ears. Using a palette knife, carefully transfer these three mice from the cooling rack to a sheet of baking parchment to set.

Re-melt the chocolate a little if needed, then repeat in batches with the rest of the mice. (If you are a quick worker, or if it's a warm day, you might be able to do six at a time, but you don't want the chocolate on the mice to harden before you've got the ears in.)

So now you have 12 blind mice with ears and noses, but no eyes or tails. Pipe little round white eyes between the nose and ears and allow the icing to set.

Now pipe chocolate dots in the middle of each white eye and pipe a chocolate swirl for the tail. Leave to set. You can put them in the fridge to speed cooling, but don't leave them there, as the chocolate will lose its shine. (Also, what sort of monster would leave mice in the fridge?)

We serve the mice in white paper cupcake cases. It looks pretty and it will also hide any imperfections in your chocolate enrobing skills.

Rum truffles

These are the grown-up version of the truffle mice on the previous page. Less cute. More alcoholic. And definitely easier to make when there are two of you in the kitchen.

Makes 12 truffles or 36 petit fours
1 batch of chocolate cake truffle mix
  (see page 91 of the truffle mice recipe)
50ml rum
170g 54% dark chocolate
150g chocolate vermicelli

Make the chocolate cake truffle mix following the truffle mouse recipe on page 91. Add the rum as you mix the other ingredients together.

Divide the mixture into 12 equal pieces. Or you could divide it into 36 smaller pieces to make mini after-dinner treats, perfect for petit fours. Roll each piece into a ball.

Melt the chocolate in a bowl very gently in the microwave (give it 20 seconds on medium and stir, then another 20 seconds until melted), or in a heatproof bowl set over a pan of barely simmering water. The aim is to just melt the chocolate, but not allow it to get hotter than 34°C so that it will stay tempered and set firm and shiny.

Tip the vermicelli into a flattish cereal bowl. We do the next stage with two people and disposable plastic gloves.

Don the disposable gloves. Person one is in charge of dipping the truffles into the melted chocolate. Hold the truffle firmly, dip it into the melted chocolate, then roll it between your hands, over the bowl so that it has a thin, even coating of chocolate (the excess can drip back into the bowl). Then drop the chocolate-coated truffle gently into the vermicelli bowl.

Person two is in charge of rolling the truffle in the vermicelli, tapping it gently on the side of the bowl to remove the excess and placing it to set on a sheet of baking parchment.

Leave to set for a few minutes on a cold day and up to 1 hour on a hot summer's day. You can put them in the fridge for a few minutes to help the process, but don't leave them there, as the chocolate will lose its shine.

Friands

Moist, buttery, delicate and topped with fresh fruit, friands are Australia's answer to the madeleine and financier, and a truly wonderful gift to the world of cake. We usually top these with blueberries and raspberries because they look so pretty, but you can choose almost any fruit. We often branch out and use whatever is in season — rhubarb, apricot and pear are all particularly good.

Makes 12 friands
200g unsalted butter
6 medium egg whites
250g icing sugar
170g ground almonds
50g plain flour
zest of 1 lemon

To decorate
blueberries
raspberries
icing sugar, for dusting

Preheat the oven to 170°C (150°C fan).

Melt the butter in a microwave or small saucepan and leave to cool. Grease a friand mould with a little of the melted butter.

Whisk the egg whites until a foam forms on the top of the whites (do not overwhisk; you are definitely not making meringues).

In a separate bowl, mix together the sugar, ground almonds, flour and lemon zest.

Fold the egg whites into the dry ingredients by hand using a large metal spoon, but do not overmix, then fold in the melted butter.

Spoon the mixture evenly into the moulds and place a couple of blueberries and a couple of raspberries on top of each friand.

Bake for 25–30 minutes until the friands are golden and spring back when touched.

Leave them to cool completely in their moulds, then carefully turn them out and dust with icing sugar.

CAKE PRINCESS: KIRSTY CHAPMAN

Kirstys is the face you're most likely to see smiling at you as you walk in the front door of Fitzbillies. She's a Cambridge girl through and through, born on Mill Road and brought up on a farm just outside of town. She took her first front-of-house job at the age of 14 and, after years of working with them, still says that Fitzbillies' regular customers are the best part of her job.

Kirsty started at Fitzbillies as a waitress in 2003 and soon became café manager, but she very quickly developed a sort of deep, anthropological understanding of the unique rhythms that affect customers. A profoundly specialised field... and very 'Cambridge'.

It was Kirsty who first observed and recorded the phenomenon of 'scone o'clock', a period on particular afternoons when cream teas become so popular that we struggle to keep up with the jam and clotted cream. In much the same way that the Vatican works out the dates for Easter, only Kirsty understands the secret signs and arcane algorithms that dictate precisely when scone o'clock will occur.

Another of her seminal discoveries was 'sunny/rainy'... the cause of our busiest days. On really sunny days customers buy cake and go and sit in the sun, on rainy days they stay at home, but on 'sunny/rainy' days they come out in force, duck into the café when the showers start and then leave the minute the rain stops. Some people have suggested that Kirsty has a secret hotline to the Met Office, but we suspect that, as a farmer's daughter, she can predict a busy day by looking at the clouds.

Kirsty spent five years working as a visual merchandiser, creating award-winning window displays for Habitat and Liberty, a talent she utilises in the constantly changing decoration of Fitzbillies' magnificent shopfront. It's because of her that visitors stop and stare through the windows and, particularly at Christmas, we find ourselves cleaning hundreds of little nose smears off the glass at child height.

What keeps such a talented person in the Fitzbillies family? 'I love our unique independent quality and style,' she says, 'how important we are to Cambridge (and I love Cambridge!)... and Gill.'

ICED CAKES

Iced cakes are the stars of the baking world. They are the centrepiece of celebrations large and small: birthdays, tea parties and, now that fruit cakes have fallen out of favour, christenings and weddings.

A few years ago, a two-layer cake with a few candles would have sufficed. But a combination of Instagram and *The Great British Bake Off* seems to have resulted in a kind of cake inflation. Three, four or even five layers are now *de rigueur*. For the recipes in this section, we've baked two fairly deep cakes and split each one horizontally to create a tall, elegant, four-tier cake, perfect for a birthday party of 10–16 people.

You could leave these cakes very plain or go mad with fresh fruit, sweets, macarons or whatever else comes to mind, depending on the occasion.

Lemon cake

*This is our most popular cake for weddings,
parties and summer celebrations. We make
it in every size – a simple iced sponge cake to
serve for tea to a five-tier wedding cake covered
with fresh fruit, roses and macarons. This recipe
will give you enough for a four-layer 18cm cake.*

330g unsalted butter (or mix of 50/50
    butter and baking margarine), softened,
    plus extra for greasing
330g caster sugar
6 medium eggs
330g self-raising flour
zest and juice of 2 lemons
fresh fruit, to decorate

For the lemon syrup
100g caster sugar
100ml water
zest and juice of 2 lemons

140g lemon curd , for the filling

For the icing
1 batch of cream cheese icing
    (see recipe on page 116)
zest of 1 lemon

Preheat the oven to 190C (170°C fan). Grease
and line the bases of two deep 18cm sandwich
or cake tins.

Cream the butter and sugar using a stand mixer
until pale and fluffy. Add the eggs, two at a time,
beating well after each addition, and then stir in
2 tablespoons of the flour to prevent it curdling.
Scrape the sides of the bowl down occasionally.
Mix in the lemon zest and juice. Then add the
rest of the flour and mix on a slow speed until
just combined. (You don't want to overwork the
gluten in the flour or knock the air out.)

Divide the mixture evenly between the two tins
and smooth with a palette knife – you can weigh
them to check that you have the same amount in
each, if you like. Bake for 25–30 minutes until
the cakes spring back to the touch. Leave in the
tins to cool completely.

To make the lemon syrup, combine the sugar,
water and the lemon zest and juice in a pan,
bring to the boil and then allow to cool.

Make the cream cheese icing according to the
recipe on page 116. Mix in the lemon zest. If the
icing is a bit soft, chill it in the fridge for 1 hour.

Trim any doming on the top of the sponges, then
slice each cake horizontally into two even layers.
Place one layer on a cake board or plate, drizzle
with syrup and spread with lemon curd. Place
the next layer on top. Drizzle with syrup, then
spread with cream cheese icing. Place the next
layer on top. Drizzle with syrup and spread with
lemon curd. Then place the last sponge layer on
top – do not add any more syrup. Coat the cake
with the rest of the cream cheese icing according
to the instructions on page 114.

We decorate our lemon cakes with fresh fruit
such as summer berries and cherries.

Coffee cake

We're lucky enough to have a constant supply of great coffee from our baristas, so we use it to make this cake. However, you could also use any type of strong coffee you can brew at home – just make it as strong as you can to get maximum coffee taste without too much liquid. Then enjoy your cake with even more coffee.

330g unsalted butter (or mix of 50/50 butter
    and baking margarine), softened, plus
    extra for greasing
330g caster sugar
6 medium eggs
330g self-raising flour
6 tbsp strong espresso coffee

For the coffee cream cheese icing
1 batch of cream cheese icing
    (see recipe on page 116)
2 tsp Camp Chicory & Coffee Essence
    (or extremely strong espresso coffee)

For the coffee syrup
100g caster sugar
2 tbsp strong espresso coffee
70ml water

chocolate-dipped coffee beans,
    to decorate

Preheat the oven to 180°C (160°C fan). Grease and line the bases of two deep 18cm sandwich or cake tins.

Cream the butter and sugar in a stand mixer until pale and fluffy. Add the eggs, two at a time, beating well and alternating with 2 tablespoons of the flour before adding the next two eggs. Scrape the bowl down after each flour addition. Add the rest of the flour and mix on a slow speed until just combined. Finally, stir in the espresso.

Divide the mixture evenly between the two tins and smooth with a palette knife – you can weigh them to check that you have the same amount in each, if you like. Bake for 25–30 minutes until the cakes spring back to the touch. Leave in the tins to cool completely.

Make the cream cheese icing according to the recipe on page 116. Add the coffee essence. If the icing is a bit soft, chill it in the fridge for 1 hour.

To make the syrup, heat the sugar, coffee and water together in a pan until the sugar is fully dissolved.

Trim any doming on the top of the sponges, then slice each cake horizontally into two even layers. Place one layer on a cake board or plate, drizzle with with some syrup, then spread with coffee cream cheese icing. Repeat with the next two layers of cake, then place the final sponge layer on top. Coat the cake with the rest of the coffee cream cheese icing according to the instructions on page 114.

We decorate our coffee cakes with chocolate-dipped coffee beans.

Chocolate cake

We have worked continuously on our chocolate cake recipe over the years. Sometimes we test four recipes on customers in the shop – the existing recipe and three new variants. The brief to the bakers is always 'more moist and less sweet'. This cake won the most recent taste test. The secret ingredient is the small amount of beetroot, which we think increases the moistness.

> *255g plain flour*
> *260g caster sugar*
> *100g light brown soft sugar*
> *50g cocoa powder*
> *1½ tsp baking powder*
> *¾ tsp bicarbonate of soda*
> *¼ tsp salt*
> *150ml sunflower oil*
> *90ml warm water*
> *90ml buttermilk*
> *3 medium eggs*
> *1½ tsp vanilla extract*
> *70g beetroot (the kind you find pre-cooked and sealed in a plastic pack in supermarkets, or you could also boil your own)*
> *butter, for greasing*
>
> *1 batch of chocolate cream cheese icing (see recipe on page 116)*
>
> *chocolate sweets, to decorate*

Preheat the oven to 180°C (160°C fan). Grease and line the bases of two deep 18cm sandwich or cake tins.

Mix together the flour, sugars, cocoa powder, baking powder, bicarbonate of soda and salt in a bowl.

Then mix together the sunflower oil, warm water, buttermilk, eggs and vanilla extract in another bowl. Add this wet mixture to the dry mixture and stir to combine.

Blitz the beetroot in a food processor into a coarse purée. But don't overdo it – you don't want it to be liquid. Add the beetroot to the batter and mix until just combined.

Divide the mixture evenly between the two tins and smooth with a palette knife – you can weigh them to check that you have the same amount in each, if you like. Bake for 25–30 minutes until the cakes spring back to the touch. Leave in the tins to cool completely.

Make the chocolate cream cheese icing according to the recipe on page 116. If the icing is a bit soft, chill it in the fridge for 1 hour.

Trim any doming on the top of the sponges, then slice each cake horizontally into two even layers. Place one layer on a cake board or plate and spread with chocolate cream cheese icing. Repeat with the next two layers of cake, then place the final sponge layer on top. Coat the cake with the rest of the chocolate cream cheese icing according to the instructions on page 114.

Decorate however you like. We love loading ours with all our favourite chocolate sweets.

Carrot cake

Our carrot cake was my favourite cake recipe for years before we reopened Fitzbillies. It's a classic of American baking – always moist, better three or four days after baking, gently spiced and not too sweet. Complemented with clouds of cream cheese icing.

340g carrots, peeled and grated
110g walnuts, chopped
110g raisins
3 medium eggs
1 ½ tsp vanilla extract
150g caster sugar
150g light brown soft sugar
185ml corn or sunflower oil
210g plain flour
1 ½ tsp baking powder
1 ½ tsp bicarbonate of soda
2 tsp cocoa powder
1 ½ tsp ground cinnamon
¾ tsp salt
butter, for greasing
1 batch of cream cheese icing (see recipe on page 116)

To decorate
20g chopped candied orange peel
20g pumpkin seeds

Preheat the oven to 175°C (155°C fan). Grease and line the bases of two deep 18cm sandwich or cake tins.

In a bowl, mix the grated carrots with the walnuts and raisins.

In another bowl, beat together the eggs, vanilla extract, sugars and oil.

Add all the flour, baking powder, bicarbonate of soda, cocoa powder, cinnamon and salt to the wet mixture and stir to combine. Tip in the carrot, walnut and raisin mix and stir again until just combined.

Divide the mixture evenly between the two tins and smooth with a palette knife – you can weigh them to check that you have the same amount in each, if you like. Bake for 35–40 minutes until the cakes spring back to the touch. Leave in the tins to cool completely. This cake gets even better overnight, or after a few days, so ideally make it the day before you attempt to ice it.

Make the cream cheese icing according to the recipe on page 116. If the icing is a bit soft, chill it in the fridge for 1 hour.

Trim any doming on the top of the sponges, then slice each cake horizontally into two even layers. Place one layer on a cake board or plate and spread with cream cheese icing. Repeat with the next two layers of cake, then place the final sponge layer on top. Coat the cake with the rest of the cream cheese icing according to the instructions on page 114.

We top our carrot cake with chopped candied orange peel and pumpkin seeds. Or sometimes we pipe little carrots on the top of each slice.

Red velvet cake

We make no apologies for putting a classic American cake in a book of English baking. We first started making this four or five years ago and it flies out of the shop as soon as we put it on the counter. Those who know it love it. Those who don't think it's a bit weird to put so much food colouring in a cake, but they are quickly converted after their first bite.

225g caster sugar

2 medium eggs

½ tsp salt

250ml sunflower oil, plus extra
    for greasing

1 ½ tsp vanilla extract

150ml buttermilk

1 ½ tsp bicarbonate of soda

2 tsp lemon juice

225g plain flour

1 ½ tbsp cocoa powder

1 tsp red food colouring paste (we use
    Sugarflair, which is available from cake-
    decorating shops and online; the liquid
    food colouring available in supermarkets
    is a bit feeble)

1 batch of cream cheese icing
    (see recipe on page 116)

Preheat the oven to 180°C (160°C fan). Grease and line the bases of two deep 18cm sandwich or cake tins.

Put the sugar, eggs and salt in the bowl of a stand mixer and whisk until pale and creamy. With the mixer still running, add the oil in a slow stream and keep whisking until the mixture thickens. Add the vanilla extract.

In a separate large bowl, mix together the buttermilk, bicarbonate of soda and lemon juice. (The mixture will bubble and double in size, then collapse down – don't be alarmed!)

Sift one third of both the flour and cocoa powder into the egg mixture and gently whisk. Then add half the buttermilk mixture and whisk again. Repeat until you've used up both mixtures, then add the red food colouring and stir one final time.

Divide the mixture evenly between the two tins and smooth with a palette knife – you can weigh them to check that you have the same amount in each, if you like. Bake for 40–45 minutes until the cakes spring back to the touch. Leave in the tins to cool completely.

Make the cream cheese icing according to the recipe on page 116. If the icing is a bit soft, chill it in the fridge for 1 hour.

Trim any doming on the top of the sponges, reserving the trimmings for decoration, then slice each cake horizontally into two even layers. Place one layer on a cake board or plate and spread with cream cheese icing. Repeat with the next two layers of cake, then place the final sponge layer on top. Coat the cake with the rest of the cream cheese icing according to the instructions on page 116. Decorate the cake with red velvet cake crumbs.

Fairy cakes

Fairy cakes or cupcakes – are they the same? Fairy cakes were the English version, smaller and with less icing than their American cousins, but we don't really distinguish. They are all about the delicious light sponge and the beautiful icing. We try to make ours special by using silky-smooth Italian meringue buttercream icing, adding fruit purées to the icing for sharp, zingy flavours or decorating them extra-specially with handmade decorations. There are a million variations from cute to sophisticated and a different type of decoration for every season and celebration.

Makes 12 cakes

220g butter (or 50/50 butter and baking margarine), softened

220g caster sugar

2 tsp vanilla extract

4 medium eggs

220g self-raising flour

4–8 tbsp full-fat milk

1 batch of Italian meringue buttercream (see recipe on page 117)

100g raspberry purée, made by blitzing fresh raspberries

100g mango purée, unsweetened from a tin

100g blueberry purée, made by blitzing fresh blueberries

Fresh raspberries, strawberries, blueberries, lime zest, etc., to decorate

Preheat the oven to 190°C (170°C fan) and put paper cases in a 12-hole muffin or cupcake tin.

Cream together the butter and sugar in a stand mixer. Add the vanilla extract and then the eggs, one at a time, adding a couple of spoonfuls of the flour after the first egg to help prevent the mixture curdling. Mix between additions.

Fold in the rest of the flour. If, once it's beaten, the sponge batter feels too thick, 'let it down' with the milk. Then spoon the mixture evenly into the 12 paper cases, trying to get it straight into the bottom of the case without leaving any residue on the sides.

Bake for 15 minutes until lightly golden and just set. Leave to cool in the tin.

Make the Italian meringue buttercream according to the instructions on page 117, then divide it evenly between three bowls. Stir a fruit purée into each – add half the purée first so that you can check the taste and texture. If the purée is a bit runny it may start to make the icing go soft, in which case stop there. Otherwise, you can gradually add the rest of the purée if you'd like a stronger taste.

Put each flavour of icing into a piping bag (or a plastic freezer bag with the corner snipped off) and pipe a swirl of icing onto the cakes. Top with fresh fruit.

Filling & icing a cake

Achieving a professional finish when you are icing a layer cake isn't too hard once you know a few tricks and practise a little. A good turntable really helps. So does having time on your side. Ideally bake your cake one day, wrap it up well overnight and ice it the next day. It will be much more manageable.

First of all, prepare your cake layers. Trim any domed tops off your sponges. Place your hand on top of one of the sponges and use a long serrated knife to cut through it horizontally, rotating as you go, to create two even layers. Repeat with the next sponge. Always keep a layer with sharp corners for the top of the cake. It's important to be able to move your fully iced cake to a cake stand or plate without damaging it, which is why in the bakery we put cakes on cake cards to decorate them. If you don't have a cake card, you could ice it directly on a cake plate, or you could use the metal base from a cake tin.

Place the bottom layer of your cake onto the cake card and then onto the turntable. Place a large spoonful of icing onto the middle of the sponge and use a palette knife to spread it gently. A small offset palette knife can make it easier. Keep moving in one direction to avoid tearing up the cake crumbs. Make sure you don't transfer cake crumbs back into the main bowl of icing. (If it's all getting a bit crumb-y, it's sometimes wise to transfer the portion of icing you are using into a small separate bowl to avoid getting crumbs in the icing that you will need to be smooth and perfect on the top of your cake.) Aim for a thin layer – if you make the icing very thick, there is a danger that the layers of cake will skate around on each other or the icing will squish out from under the weight of the cake. Place the next layer on top, orientating it strategically to correct any sloping or unevenness of height. Add a layer of icing. Keep going until you put the top layer on.

Now you are going to crumb-coat the cake. This involves putting a very thin layer of icing all over the cake, top and sides, to seal in the crumbs, so that when you apply the outer layer of icing, it will look perfect, untainted by crumbs. Start by putting a very thin layer of icing on the top of the cake. It doesn't matter if you can see cake through it, or if it is thicker in some places to fill dents or uneven height. Now apply icing to the side of the cake. Again, you are going for a very thin, almost transparent coating. Keep going all round the cake, rotating the turntable. Once the sides are covered, take a long palette knife and hold it vertically against the cake, at a 45-degree angle, and rotate the turntable so that the knife removes the excess icing and leaves a smooth side. This will cause some of the icing to stand up around the edge, above the top of the cake – use the palette knife to smooth it into the top of the cake. Leave the crumb-coated cake to set for an hour. Put it in the fridge if it's a very warm day.

Now repeat with your top coat of icing. Go a little thicker this time to make sure you get a nice opaque coat. Do the top first, then the sides. We would then finish the cake with a swirl – gradually bring the palette knife out from the middle of the cake as you rotate the turntable.

Cream cheese icing

This recipe makes quite a lot of icing, so if you are just icing the middle and top of your cake, making a two-layer cake or making some cupcakes, you could just make half the batch.

Makes enough to fill, crumb coat and cover
a four-layer 18cm cake or 24 cupcakes
750g icing sugar
300g cream cheese
75g unsalted butter, very soft

For the variations
1 tsp vanilla extract
zest and juice of 1 lemon
1 tbsp extra-strong espresso

Sift the icing sugar into the bowl of a stand mixer.

Add the cream cheese, butter and any flavourings of your choice.

Put a tea towel over the mixer and start on a slow speed so that you don't make a snowstorm in the kitchen. Mix until combined.

If the icing has a good texture, you can start icing as soon as the cake is completely cold. If it seems a bit soft, put it in the fridge for an hour.

Chocolate cream cheese icing

This is an easy-to-make, easy-to-use, delicious icing. Chocolatey enough, but not so bitter so as to be off-putting to children.

Makes enough to fill, crumb coat and cover
a four-layer 18cm cake or 24 cupcakes
220g unsalted butter, very soft
150g cream cheese
100g cocoa powder
1 tsp vanilla extract
560g icing sugar
180ml full-fat milk

Mix together the butter and cream cheese in a stand mixer until combined, but don't overdo it.

Sift in the cocoa powder, then add the vanilla extract and sift in the icing sugar and beat together until combined (put a tea towel over the mixer and start slowly to avoid a snowstorm).

Add the milk gradually to get to a good spreadable texture. It should take all the milk.

If the icing has a good texture, you can start icing as soon as the cake is completely cold. If it seems a bit soft, put it in the fridge for an hour.

Italian meringue buttercream

This is a smooth, silky, unctuous buttercream. It's a very different beast from the American buttercream we are used to, where you just mix butter and icing sugar and are left with a slightly gritty texture, and it can be flavoured and coloured in all sorts of ways: lemon juice, fruit purées – try raspberry or mango – strong coffee, praline. For us, it is a bakery staple that we use in all manner of cakes.

Makes enough to fill, crumb coat and cover
a four-layer 18cm cake or 24 cupcakes
360g caster sugar
100ml water
6 medium egg whites
500g unsalted butter, softened

Put the sugar with water in a large saucepan and stir to mix.

Bring to the boil on a high heat. Use a probe or sugar thermometer and keep cooking until it reaches 120°C (this is also called the soft ball stage), then remove from the heat.

While the sugar syrup is heating, put the egg whites in the bowl of a stand mixer (check the bowl and whisk attachment are very clean – scald them with boiling water if necessary and make sure that no speck of egg yolk has got into the whites). Whisk to soft peaks.

Keep the mixer running and pour the sugar syrup into the egg whites in a slow, steady stream. Be careful not to hit the whisk or the side of the bowl, as the sugar will set on them. Continue whisking until the meringue has cooled slightly.

Add the butter, a third at a time, and whisk until fully incorporated.

Keep in a covered bowl at room temperature until you need it. It will keep well for about a week at room temperature. There is no need to refrigerate it.

TRAYBAKES

Although the 'traybake' might seem to be a modern phenomenon*, traditional bakers have been baking things in trays for years — they just appear on British menus as 'slices': cherry slice, apple slice, coconut slice and so on. In the US they are known as 'bar cookies' or 'sheet cakes' and include brownies and flapjacks. They are an amazingly convenient way of feeding a lot of people — none other than St Mary Berry suggests that traybakes are 'ideal for cricket teas' — and they remain popular at church and other social events.

With the sudden rise in coffee culture, traybakes really come into their own. Sliced into convenient servings, they are the 'go-to' accompaniment to a good cup of coffee and it doesn't take too much addition of oats and dried fruit to turn them into something worryingly healthy — or at least something you might eat for breakfast with minimal guilt.

* First reference in the UK mainstream press as a single word is in *The Grocer* in 2001

Date slice

The date slice may not be our most glamorous-looking cake – it looks a bit brown, oaty and possibly rather worthy – but it is one of our most popular and has been for years. Lots of our regulars tell us it's their favourite and every time we eat a slice we remember why. Gill reckons it's the very best cake to take on a picnic.

Makes 12 bars (or 24 mini bars)
340g pitted dates
50g caster sugar
100g plain flour
160g wholemeal flour
160g jumbo oats
50g desiccated coconut
1 tsp salt
190g sunflower margarine or unsalted butter,
  cold, plus extra for greasing

Preheat the oven to 185°C (165°C fan). Grease and line the base and sides of a 30cm x 20cm traybake tin.

Put the dates and caster sugar in a pan and just cover with water. Cook until soft (about 10 minutes), stirring occasionally. Be careful not to let them catch on the bottom of the pan. Put to one side.

Mix all the dry ingredients in a bowl.

Add the sunflower margarine or butter and rub in with your fingertips to form a crumble.

Put half the crumble mixture into the tin and press down flat with the palm of your hand.

Spoon the date mixture onto the crumble base and spread with a palette knife.

Sprinkle the rest of the crumble mixture on top. Press it down gently, but not too much, so that it stays nice and crumbly.

Bake for 35–40 minutes until golden.

Allow to cool completely in the tin, then cut into 12 bars (or 24 mini portions).

Chocolate brownies

When we first reopened Fitzbillies in 2011 we didn't make brownies. We tried to be terribly purist and only make traditional British cakes. Brownies, we felt, were too American for a 90-year-old English cake shop. But every day customers asked for brownies. Then our daughter (nine years old at the time) demanded them. With her help we tested lots of recipes, found the one she liked best and we've never looked back.

Makes 12 brownies (or 24 mini brownies)
250g 70% dark chocolate
220g unsalted butter, plus extra for greasing
140g plain flour
400g caster sugar
4 large eggs , beaten

Preheat the oven to 175°C (155°C fan). Grease and line the base and sides of a 30cm x 20cm traybake tin.

Melt the chocolate and the butter in a microwave or pan until melted and stir together. (Start with 30 seconds on medium in the microwave, then stir and do another 20 or 30 seconds. Repeat until melted.)

Transfer to a large bowl, stir in the flour and sugar and mix until just combined. Then stir in the eggs until thick and smooth.

Pour the mixture into the lined tin and bake for 25–30 minutes until just set. Do not overbake.

Allow to cool completely in the tin. Then cut into 12 portions (or 24 mini brownies) with a sharp knife, wiping it with a hot (clean) cloth between cuts if needed.

Duke of Cambridge cake

This recipe is based on the recipe published by Darren McGrady, the Royal Chef. It is the cake that the palace chefs made for Prince William when he was a child and that he chose for his own wedding cake (alongside the traditional white cake) when he married Catherine Middleton. Prince William and Catherine were married in 2011, at around the same time we were reopening Fitzbillies. On their marriage, they were given the titles of Duke and Duchess of Cambridge. So we decided to honour them the way we do best – with cake.

Makes 10 bars
340g Rich Tea biscuits
250g 70% dark chocolate
130g unsalted butter, at room temperature,
    plus extra for greasing
130g caster sugar
150g 54% dark chocolate

Grease and line the base and sides of a 30cm x 20cm traybake tin.

Break the biscuits into almond-sized pieces. Don't blitz them in a food processor, as they will turn to crumbs and you need decent-sized pieces.

Melt the 70% chocolate in the microwave (give it 20 seconds on medium and stir, then another 20 seconds until melted), or in a heatproof bowl set over a pan of barely simmering water.

Cream the butter and sugar in a stand mixer until pale and fluffy. Add the melted chocolate and mix well.

Add the biscuits, a handful at a time, stirring gently so that you don't break them up too much, but enough that they get completely coated with the chocolate mixture. Tip the mixture into the prepared tin and press down. (We cover the mixture with a sheet of baking parchment and smooth over the top of that.) Chill in the fridge overnight or for at least 4 hours.

Let the biscuit base come back to room temperature while you melt the 54% chocolate in the same way you did previously. (Your objective is not to let it get above 34°C so that it will stay tempered and give a nice shiny finish.)

Pour the melted chocolate onto the biscuit base and spread quickly with a palette knife. Allow to set at room temperature, then cut into 10 bars with a sharp knife.

Shortbread

Shortbread is perhaps the simplest of all baking. So it has to be perfect. With a good recipe, you can make fingers, shortbread rounds or petticoat tails. At Christmas, we like to make walnut shortbread and pack it in pretty boxes for gifts.

Makes 24 fingers or rounds
185g unsalted butter, softened
100g caster sugar, plus extra for sprinkling
generous pinch of salt
270g plain flour, plus extra for dusting
   if you are making biscuit shapes
25g ground rice
demerara sugar, if you are rolling
   round biscuits

For walnut shortbread
100g walnuts, chopped

Preheat the oven to 180°C (160°C fan). If making shortbread fingers, grease and line a 30cm x 20cm traybake tin. Alternatively, if you are making round shortbread biscuits or other shapes, line baking sheets with baking parchment.

Cream the butter, sugar and salt in a large bowl until well mixed (but not to the pale and fluffy stage). Add the flour and ground rice and mix until just combined. Add the chopped walnuts at this stage if you are making walnut shortbread.

If making shortbread fingers, press the mixture firmly into the baking tin with the palm of your hand and prick it all over with a fork.

If making round shortbread biscuits, roll the dough into a fat sausage, then roll the sausage in demerara sugar, wrap it in cling film and chill in the fridge for 1 hour. When you take it out of the fridge, remove the cling film and use a sharp knife to cut 1cm-thick rounds of shortbread. Place these, spaced apart, on lined baking sheets.

If making shortbread shapes, like the shortbread hearts we have in the shop, roll the dough out on a lightly floured surface to 6mm thick and cut out shapes using your desired cutter. Repeat with any leftover dough. Place these, spaced apart, on lined baking sheets.

Bake the shortbread until golden for about 25 minutes for shortbread fingers, 12 minutes for round biscuits and 8–10 minutes for shortbread hearts or other shapes.

When baked, remove from the oven, transfer to a cooling rack and sprinkle with caster sugar. If making shortbread fingers, slice in the tin before transferring to the cooling rack.

Millionaire's shortbread

We only started making millionaire's shortbread recently. We always felt we had too many chocolate traybakes already, and as you can buy it pretty much anywhere, did the world really need another version? The answer is unequivocally 'yes' – as soon as we started testing recipes, we found that whole trays of it just disappeared in the bakery. If we loved it so much, so would our customers. Now we make it at the weekends when we feel a special treat is in order.

> Makes 12 fingers or 24 squares
> *1 batch of shortbread (see recipe on page 127)*
> *200g unsalted butter*
> *397g tin condensed milk*
> *100g golden syrup*
> *60g milk chocolate*
> *80g 54% dark chocolate*
> *70g double cream*
> *¼ tsp salt*

Bake the shortbread in a deep-sided, lined baking tin according to the recipe on page 127. Leave it to cool completely in the tin.

Put the butter, condensed milk and golden syrup into a microwaveable bowl. Heat in the microwave for 7 minutes on high heat, taking it out after every minute to stir well. Alternatively, heat in a saucepan over a low heat. When it is ready it will look thicker and darker in colour.

Pour the caramel mixture onto the shortbread and leave to cool.

Melt both chocolates together in one bowl very gently in the microwave (give it 20 seconds on medium and stir, then another 20 seconds until melted), or in a heatproof bowl set over a pan of barely simmering water. The aim is to just melt the chocolate, but not allow it to get hotter than 34°C so that it will stay tempered and set firm and shiny. Add the double cream to the melted chocolate and stir until combined.

Sprinkle the salt over the caramel. Pour the chocolate mixture carefully all over the caramel. Quickly use a palette knife to fill any gaps before it starts to set. Leave to cool, but don't put it in the fridge or it will go too hard to cut and you will lose the gloss on the chocolate.

Use a sharp knife to cut into 24 fingers or 12 squares. Wipe the knife between each cut to get a clean finish.

Clementine & cranberry slice

This is a deliciously moist and colourful cake. The clementines are boiled whole, so we like to think it's one of our five a day, and it's gluten-free. It gets even better a few days after baking.

Makes 12 finger slices
420g whole clementines, about 4
6 medium eggs
230g caster sugar
250g ground almonds
1 tsp gluten-free baking powder
110g dried cranberries
butter, baking margarine or oil spray,
    for greasing

Put the clementines in a saucepan, cover with water and cook on medium heat for 2 hours. Top up the water if needed or keep a lid on the pan. Drain and leave to cool. It's a good idea to do this the night before you intend to bake.

When the clementines are cool, blitz them in a food processor, skins and all.

Preheat the oven to 180°C (160°C fan) and grease and line a 30cm x 20cm traybake tin.

Beat the eggs gently in a bowl and then add the caster sugar, ground almonds and baking powder and mix to combine.

Add the clementine pulp and mix to combine.

Pour the mixture into the prepared tin and scatter the cranberries over the top.

Bake for 30–35 minutes until the cake springs back to the touch. Leave to cool in the tin, then cut into 12 fingers with a sharp knife.

White chocolate & raspberry blondie

We make this blondie as a weekend special in the summer. Everyone loves it – white chocolate lovers and those who usually eschew it alike. The sharpness of the raspberries counteracts the usual tendency of white chocolate to be cloying.

Makes 12 slices
215g unsalted butter, plus extra for greasing
375g white chocolate, buttons or
   broken into pieces
4 medium eggs
215g white granulated sugar
235g plain flour
215g fresh raspberries
zest of 1 orange

Preheat the oven to 180°C (160°C fan) and grease and line a 30cm x 20cm traybake tin.

Melt the butter and half the white chocolate together in one bowl very gently in the microwave (give it 20 seconds on medium and stir, then another 20 seconds until melted), or in a heatproof bowl set over a pan of barely simmering water.

Whisk the eggs and sugar together in a large bowl until creamy and slightly thickened and then whisk in the butter and chocolate mixture.

Sift in the flour and mix until just combined.

Add half the remaining white chocolate, half the raspberries and all the orange zest and mix gently by hand.

Turn the mixture into the prepared baking tin and spread out gently with a spatula.

Sprinkle the remaining chocolate and raspberries on the top.

Bake for 35 minutes until just set and turning golden. Do not overbake or you will lose the squishy texture. Leave to cool in the tin, then cut into 12 fingers with a sharp knife.

PASTRIES

With a sweet pastry shell the options are limitless – you can make it into anything from a homely apple pie to a glamorous strawberry tart.

In the bakery we think about bases (sponge cakes, pastry, etc.) and creams or fillings. The tart is perhaps the best example of how this approach gives you dozens of promising combinations.

Our pastry recipe is buttery and short, but relatively easy to work with. We use it for full-size tarts to be cut into slices, individual tartlets and mini tart cases for the beautiful fruit tarts for our afternoon teas.

Then there's the choice of filling: crème pâtissière topped with fresh berries, frangipane, simple baked fruits, chocolate, caramel, lemon...

Plum & ricotta tart

We called this plum and ricotta tart, but we could equally have called it apricot and ricotta, rhubarb and ricotta, gooseberry and ricotta and so on, because the sweet pastry and gentle taste of the ricotta filling make a wonderful backdrop for whatever fruit is in season. Just choose your favourite.

1 batch of sweet pastry
 (see the recipe on page 146)
90g unsalted butter, softened,
 plus extra for greasing
165g caster sugar
½ tsp vanilla extract
3 medium eggs, separated
180g ground almonds
zest and juice of 2 lemons
225g ricotta
8 plums, stoned and sliced
plain flour, for dusting
apricot jam, strained and boiled,
 for glazing (optional)

Make a batch of sweet pastry using the recipe on page 146. Chill in the fridge for an hour or more.

Preheat the oven to 180°C (160°C fan) and grease and flour a 28cm tart tin.

Remove the pastry from the fridge. If it's been in there a long time, i.e. overnight, get it out half an hour before so that it comes to room temperature. Lightly flour a surface and roll out the pastry until it's a few inches wider than the tin. Ensure it doesn't stick by moving it around gently as you work and keeping the surface well floured.

Roll the pastry over the rolling pin and then place it over the tart tin. Gently press into the sides, then trim the top edge all the way around with a sharp knife. Prick the base with a fork. Blind bake for 15–20 minutes until lightly golden – you don't want to overbake the edges, but nor do you want a soggy bottom.

Reduce the oven temperature to 175°C (155°C fan).

Cream the butter, sugar and vanilla extract in a stand mixer until pale and fluffy. Add the egg yolks, one at a time, mixing after each addition, then add the ground almonds and lemon zest and juice and mix again. Fold in the ricotta by hand.

Whisk the egg whites in a separate bowl until stiff. Gently fold them into the egg yolk mixture, then spoon the mix into the pastry case, spreading it gently to make an even layer.

Top with the sliced plums, carefully arranged in pretty circles.

Bake for 45 minutes until the plums are soft and the ricotta mix is slightly puffed up and light golden in colour. When cool, you can brush with an apricot jam glaze or serve just as it is.

Apple crumble tart

Which is better: apple tart or apple crumble?
At Fitzbillies you'll never have to choose.
A sweet pastry base, filled with sharp Bramley
apples and topped with a buttery, gently spiced
crumble. The only question is whether to add ice
cream or clotted cream.

> *1 batch of sweet pastry*
> *(see recipe on page 146)*
> *1.2kg Bramley apples, about 4 large apples*
> *juice of 1 lemon*
> *100g breadcrumbs*
> *170g plain flour, plus extra for dusting*
> *50g caster sugar*
> *50g demerara sugar*
> *1 ¼ tsp mixed spice*
> *70g rolled oats*
> *150g unsalted butter, cold, plus extra*
> *for greasing*
> *ice cream or clotted cream, to serve*

Make a batch of sweet pastry using the recipe on page 146. Chill in the fridge for an hour or more.

Preheat the oven to 185°C (165°C fan) and grease and flour a large 28cm tart tin.

Remove the pastry from the fridge. If it's been in there a long time, i.e. overnight, get it out half an hour before so that it comes to room temperature. Lightly flour a surface and roll out the pastry until it's a few inches wider than the tin. Ensure it doesn't stick by moving it around gently as you work and keeping the surface well floured.

Roll the pastry over the rolling pin and then place it over the tart tin. Gently press into the sides, then trim the top edge all the way around with a sharp knife. Prick the base with a fork. Blind bake for 15–20 minutes until lightly golden – you don't want to overbake the edges, but nor do you want a soggy bottom.

Now peel, core and thinly slice the apples, then place them in a bowl. Mix in the lemon juice – it's partly for taste and partly to stop the apples turning brown.

Sprinkle the breadcrumbs into the base of the pastry case (they will absorb the apple juice and stop the pastry going soggy).

Now make the crumble mix. Put the flour, both sugars, mixed spice and oats in a bowl. Then rub the butter roughly into the dry ingredients, so that you get nice crumbly chunks.

Place the apples in layers into the pasty case on top of the breadcrumbs.

Sprinkle the crumble mixture on top. Gently spread it around so that it's even, but do not press down.

Bake in the oven for 40–45 minutes until the crumble is golden brown. Serve warm or cold with ice cream or clotted cream.

Bakewell tart

Bakewell tart plays a very important role in our story. This is the tart we took to the pitch meeting with our landlords and the cake we firmly believe won us Fitzbillies.

We got up early that morning to make this recipe. Not a stodgy, old-style Bakewell tart, over-sweet and with lots of fondant icing, but a light, buttery frangipane, with the sharpness of French raspberries. We intended it as a metaphor to explain how we would take something old, traditional and with a lot of history, but which had lost its relevance for the modern age, and reinvent it, keeping the heritage, yet making it even better and appealing to contemporary tastes. Here's a Bakewell tart — just as good (maybe better) than the frangipane tarts of French pâtisserie.

1 batch of sweet pastry
   (see recipe on page 146)
6 medium eggs
250g caster sugar
250g ground almonds
250g unsalted butter, melted,
   plus extra for greasing
100g raspberry jam
125g fresh raspberries
30g flaked almonds
plain flour, for dusting

Make a batch of sweet pastry using the recipe on page 146. Chill in the fridge for an hour or more.

Preheat the oven to 185°C (165°C fan) and grease and flour a loose-bottomed 28cm tart tin.

Beat together the eggs and sugar in a bowl until pale and fluffy. Add the ground almonds and melted butter and mix until combined.

Remove the pastry from the fridge. If it's been in there a long time, i.e. overnight, get it out half an hour before so that it comes to room temperature. Lightly flour a surface and roll out the pastry until it's a few inches wider than the tin. Ensure it doesn't stick by moving it around gently as you work and keeping the surface well floured.

Roll the pastry over the rolling pin and then place it over the tart tin. Gently press into the sides, then trim the top edge all the way around with a sharp knife. Prick the base with a fork. Blind bake for 15–20 minutes until lightly golden — you don't want to overbake the edges, but nor do you want a soggy bottom.

Spread the raspberry jam onto the base of the tart and sprinkle the whole raspberries over it. Pour the almond mixture over the jam and raspberries, then sprinkle with the flaked almonds.

Put the tart in the oven (on a baking sheet in case of any overflowing or spills) and bake for 40 minutes until the mixture rises and is golden. Serve warm or cold, with clotted cream.

Fresh fruit tart

These tarts are the precious jewels of the bakery world. The bright, translucent colours of the fruit look so beautiful and they taste so fresh. People who say they don't like cake like these tarts. So simple: pastry, custard, fruit. So perfect: these tarts always make the cut as part of our afternoon teas.

Makes 12 individual small tarts
1 batch of sweet pastry
(see recipe on page 146)

For the crème pâtissière
300ml full-fat milk
1 tsp vanilla bean paste
3 medium egg yolks
50g caster sugar
2 tbsp cornflour
2 tbsp plain flour

fresh strawberries, raspberries, redcurrants,
* sliced peaches, cherries, mint leaves, etc,*
* for topping*
apricot jam, for glazing (optional)
butter or cooking oil, for greasing

Put the milk in a thick-bottomed saucepan, add the vanilla bean paste and bring to the boil. Leave to cool a little.

Put the egg yolks in a bowl (save the whites for making meringues) and whisk in the caster sugar. Add the cornflour and plain flour and mix to combine, then whisk in the warm milk.

Clean the pan, then strain the crème pâtissière mixture back into it. Bring to the boil, stirring continuously until thickened.

Pour into a bowl and immediately cover the top with a piece of cling film – the cling film needs to be touching the surface of the crème pâtissière to stop a skin forming. Let it cool completely, then refrigerate.

Preheat the oven to 190°C (170°C fan). Grease and flour 12 small tart tins. You could also use the holes of a muffin or cupcake tray – these will make smaller, deeper tarts, so less room for decoration.

Now make your tarts cases. Remove the pastry from the fridge. If it's been in there a long time, i.e. overnight, get it out half an hour before so that it comes to room temperature. Lightly flour a surface and roll out the pastry. Ensure it doesn't stick by moving it around gently as you work and keeping the surface well floured.

Using a cutter slightly larger than your tart tins, cut out 12 suitably sized circles and gently press them into the bases and sides of the tins. Trim the top edges all the way around with a sharp knife and prick the bases with a fork. Blind bake for 15 minutes until lightly golden – you don't want to overbake the edges, but nor do you want a soggy bottom. Leave to cool completely.

RECIPE CONTINUED OVERLEAF

Sweet pastry

Fill the bottoms of the tart cases with the crème pâtissière. We usually make a lot, so we use a piping bag, but spreading with the back of a spoon works fine too.

Go mad topping them with fresh berries, sliced fruit and mint leaves.

If you are serving the tarts immediately, they will be fine just as they are. If you want to serve them the next day or add a bit of gloss, you can glaze the tarts with some warmed apricot jam (add a teaspoon of boiling water if it seems overly thick).

This pastry is a very traditional sweet pastry recipe. It's been used at Fitzbillies for at least 50 years, probably longer. It's pretty much what every British high-street baker would have used, as it's easy to work with and flexible. We make a giant batch and store it until we need it.

Makes enough for a single 28cm tart
or 12 individual small tarts
85g unsalted butter
85g baking margarine
60g caster sugar
1 medium egg, beaten
255g plain flour, plus extra for dusting
¼ tsp salt

Mix together the butter, margarine and caster sugar in a bowl, but do not cream. Mix in the egg.

Add the flour and salt and mix until combined. If it doesn't come together after a minute, add a little water (a teaspoon at a time) until it does come together.

Form into a ball, wrap in cling film and chill for an hour before use.

CHAIRMAN & JANITOR: TIM HAYWARD

Tim Hayward has the best and worst job at Fitzbillies. He is chairman and janitor, public face and private dogsbody.

On a good day, he jumps into his tiny sports car, drives to one of the branches of Fitzbillies to high-five the baristas and picks up (probably) the best coffee in town. He chucks a few babies under the chin, tastes something the chefs made earlier, sits in the window seat to dash off an opinion piece for the papers and then heads to the station to go to London to pick up an award or review a restaurant. That's a good day… maybe one day in ten.

On a bad day, his phone rings at 4am. Break-in at one of the cafés? Power gone at the bakery? He heaves himself into a less-glamorous car with a bootful of tools for every eventuality and goes off to board up a window or reset the power. Every day, somewhere at Fitzbillies there's a power outage, blocked toilet, lost internet connection, broken lock, leaking coffee machine. That's business as usual. And Tim keeps the show on the road. (There's probably a Tim in every thriving small business. You don't thrive without one.)

He's also our graphic designer, photographer and IT expert, setting up and managing the ever-larger number of cloud-hosted software systems that keep the business running – the tills, card machines, accounts system, HR system, ordering system. If you ring him up to tell him it's broken, he will tell you to switch it off and back on again. It usually works.

You won't find Tim studying a spreadsheet, writing a health and safety policy or conducting a staff review – he doesn't really trouble modern management practice – but you will find him bringing a uniquely qualified view of where the hospitality industry is going or ideas for a new dish, and he always has time to help the people who help us most: the dedicated, professional bakers, chefs, managers, baristas and waiters in our business.

Tim challenges our orthodoxies, calms our panics, puts sticking plaster on our scraped knees and, with an unfathomable combination of enthusiasm and grumpiness, picks us up ready to open the business again for another day.

SAVOURIES

Bakery savouries were the original fast food. Pie shops have been around since the Middle Ages, and right up until the invention of the packet sandwich in the 1980s and the arrival of fast-food chains, they were the best option for a quick takeaway lunch.

The favourites are remarkably unchanged since the 1930s. Sausage rolls top the list. We make our own sausage meat from minced pork and a special mix of spices. Served warm from the 'piequarium' (as Tim likes to call the glass-fronted pie-warming cabinet), they are irresistible. Pasties are the other great delight — braised beef with lots of root vegetables in a light shortcrust pastry.

A slightly more modern innovation is the 'savoury tart'. Most people would just call it a quiche, but in the early days of reopening Fitzbillies we were desperate to use British names rather than French, and so savoury tart has stuck. The flavour changes daily, different combinations of vegetables and cheeses, depending on what's in season, in an unctuous egg and cream filling.

Sausage rolls

Other items might have claim to be Fitzbillies' signature dish, but our sausage rolls have an almost cult-like following, particularly amongst local tradespeople. Throughout the entire time we were closed for the renovation, white vans would pull up outside, every chippy, plumber or electrician anxiously asking when they'd be back on the counter.

We confess we were baffled. We love a sausage roll as much as the next greedy person, but this was something quite exceptional. What could the secret possibly be? We searched through the recipes we'd inherited but couldn't find anything. There was no record in the accounts of any mysterious deliveries of an arcane spice or addictive chemical, regardless, it seemed fairly clear we'd have to make a stonking sausage roll.

When head baker Gill Abbs returned to the business, it was the first thing we asked her (well, once she'd dictated the recipe for the Chelseas). Gill was, it turns out, a bit bemused. There was no secret to the sausage rolls – apart from making them fresh every day and serving them hot from the counter.

Thomas, our friend and advisor, was delighted by this. 'You'll need a Piequarium,' he said... and he was right. Those old-fashioned heated glass display cabinets that are still a fixture in greasy spoons and chippies, turned out to be perfect not only for holding warm food at safe temperatures, but also for keeping the juices of the pork filling deliciously liquid. The cabinet also lets the astonishing amount of butter in the pastry jacket properly intermingle for maximum luxurious voluptuousness.

How we make ours

We use a 'sheeter' (page 45) for the continuous and repeated rolling involved for making puff pastry, but it's a pain to make puff pastry in a domestic kitchen. Fortunately, the stuff you can buy ready-made and chilled at the supermarket is extremely good, but make sure you buy the all-butter version.

You need a long shape for efficiency. In the bakery, this is done with the dough straight out of the sheeter and placed directly onto a long table; so, on a good day, we're looking at a 3m ribbon of delicious, buttery pastry.

The filling starts with high-grade minced pork, prepared for us by our butcher. Don't be tempted to chop your own in a food processor – you need mince for the proper texture. It's also important that it's a good mix of flavourful cuts and fat. We specify a 50/50 mix of belly pork and shoulder.

We shouldn't reveal our seasoning, which we created especially, but if you stuck to the traditional British pork butcher's mix, you would be very, very close to what we use. The butcher's mix is a time-honoured blend of 3lb salt, 1lb white pepper, 10z ground nutmeg and 10z ground ginger. OK... we admit that's probably more than you're going to need, but you get the idea. It's an instantly recognisable taste to anyone with a love for pork pies, haslet or traditional butcher's sausage and, in its modest way, is as characteristic of British cookery as *ras el hanout* is of Moroccan.

For every 500g of minced pork, we add 300g of breadcrumbs. As you can imagine, a bakery traditionally produced a lot of breadcrumbs as a by-product and the sausage roll used them up. You though, like us, might want to buy some panko. Panko is a Japanese breadcrumb used for coating fried products because it absorbs any excess oil, which, in the case of sausage meat, is exactly what you want. The breadcrumbs, also referred to as 'rusk' in commercial sausage making, absorb the delicious fat and juices in the mince so that they don't leak out during cooking and go to waste. Panko does the job brilliantly.

As you can see, there's no secret (except maybe the seasoning). The rolls will be light, crispy and flaky, and are best warm, but remember that for the most truly addictive experience they need to have been held in a gently warm environment for a while, so all the flavours and textures can really get comfortable with themselves.*

---

* This is less of a cook's tip than a greedy eater's experience. Sausage rolls, like lardy cake and fresh doughnuts, should be served in a paper bag. If the bag has not gone transparent by the time you reach the door, you have inadvertently been served the low-calorie 'health' version – which you should return immediately and exchange for the real thing.

Sausage rolls

Makes 8 sausage rolls
500g minced pork
(ask your butcher for a roughly
50/50 mix of belly and shoulder)
300g panko breadcrumbs
10g salt
4g ground white pepper
⅓ tsp grated nutmeg
⅓ tsp ground ginger
1 pack ready-made all-butter
puff pastry, about 320–375g
egg, for egg washing

Preheat your oven to 210°C (190°C fan).

Mix the pork with the breadcrumbs and seasonings in a large bowl or ideally with a stand mixer. Wrap the sausage meat in cling film and refrigerate for an hour or so.

Roll out the puff pastry lengthways on a lightly floured surface. Try to keep it cool and don't overwork it. Slice the pastry in half down its length to produce two strips.

Lay one of the pastry strips along the surface in front of you and gently roll or press out the long edge nearest to you to thin it slightly.

With your hands, mould half the sausage meat into a long snake along the middle of the strip of dough. Cooking times will vary if you make the rolls fatter or thinner, so, unless you have a probe thermometer, stick to a thickness of roughly 5cm for the finished roll.

Paint the thinner edge nearest to you with water or the egg wash. Roll the pastry around the meat, pulling the far, long side towards you, tucking it down under the meat and rolling the whole thing over so that it seals where the pastry is thinned and wet. Finish when the roll is resting on the overlap.

Make a neat line of marks along the top surface with the back of a knife. These are not like the cuts you see in a loaf; they just slightly 'pinch' the puff pastry down to create an attractive traditional pattern. Brush the top surface with the egg wash and then pause to experience the simple majesty of your work. Repeat with the other strip of pastry and the remaining sausage meat.

Cut the rolls into whatever lengths please you most. At this point you can freeze any number of your batch to defrost and bake another day.

Line a baking tray with baking parchment and put the rolls on the tray. Put the tray into the oven and immediately reduce the temperature to 180°C (160°C fan). After 20 minutes, check to see that the surface of the rolls is taking on a good colour. They will be done at 40 minutes. If you want to vary the thickness, adjust the cooking time accordingly and check for a 75°C core temp with your probe thermometer.

Vegetarian sausage roll

Makes 8 sausage rolls

1kg spinach

50g unsalted butter

3 shallots, finely diced

500g chestnut mushrooms,
    coarsely chopped

3 garlic cloves, crushed or grated

250g ricotta

zest of 2 lemons

grated nutmeg, to taste

salt, to taste

ground white pepper, to taste

2 medium egg yolks, plus 1 beaten egg for
    egg washing

1 pack ready-made all-butter puff pastry,
    about 320–375g

Blanch the spinach in boiling water or steam it until it wilts. Plunge into cold water to stop it cooking, then vigorously squeeze out as much water from it as you can manage.

Melt the butter in a frying pan and soften the shallots. Add the mushrooms and garlic, then put a lid on the pan and let everything sweat nicely on a medium heat. Once the mushrooms have softened, remove the lid and continue cooking to drive off extra moisture.

Take the pan off the heat. Roughly chop the spinach and stir it in, followed by the ricotta and seasonings. Taste and adjust. Now stir in the egg yolks. Allow to cool, then cover with cling film and refrigerate for an hour or so.

Follow the assembly method for the meat sausage rolls on page 155, using this mixture instead of the sausage meat. Veggie sausage rolls are easier to handle when cold, so it's a good idea to pop them in the fridge for an hour before slicing. At this stage you can also freeze them for cooking at a later date.

Preheat the oven to 195°C (175°C fan). The veggie filling is already cooked, so just 20 minutes of cooking time until the pastry is well coloured will do the trick beautifully.

Shortcrust pastry

To keep pastry light you need to work it as little as possible, so keep your hands out of the mixture for as long as you can – as soon as you get your fingers in there, the butter will begin to melt and the resulting pastry will be less light. Grating the butter is a bit of a messy process, but it helps if you put it in the freezer for a while so it hardens.

Makes 1kg
250g unsalted butter, from the freezer
500g plain flour
⅓ tsp salt
250ml cold water

Grate the butter into your mixing bowl. Use the biggest holes on a box grater. Anything else will turn the butter into mush and what we're trying to achieve is regular-sized 'grains' of butter to distribute throughout the pastry.

Add the flour and salt and stir through with a silicone spatula to combine into a loose, crumbly texture.

Add the water and mix until combined. This is the point at which you can briefly use your hands if you're not working with a mixer.

Shape into a ball, wrap tightly in cling film and chill for 1 hour or overnight before use.

Savoury tart

We love to ring the changes on the flavours of our savoury tart day by day. There are infinite ways to vary things, but it's worth remembering this simple rule – that most tarts work well with one main vegetable, one aromatic element and one cheese in the filling. Also bear in mind that if you're messing with sizes, 1 medium egg will set 200g of cream, and 200g of cheese to 1.2 litres of cream makes a good strong cheesy flavour.

We make all our tarts as vegetarian, but there's nothing stopping you adding smoked bacon chunks, chorizo, ham or any other meaty element that takes your creative fancy.

500g (½ batch) of shortcrust pastry
  (see recipe on page 157) – alternatively,
  make a full batch and store half in the
  freezer for a later date
6 medium eggs
1.2 litres double cream
salt and pepper
butter, for greasing
plain flour, for dusting

Filling flavours

Spinach, lemon & ricotta:
200g (1 bag) baby leaf spinach, wilted
  and drained
zest of 1 lemon
50g ricotta

Mushroom, asparagus & taleggio:
100g mushrooms, sliced and quickly fried
  in butter until soft
100g asparagus, steamed and cut into chunks
200g taleggio, chopped into rough slices

Onion, marjoram & goats' cheese:
2 red onions, roasted whole in their skins
  at 170ºC (150ºC) for 30 minutes,
  then tough outer leaves peeled off,
  the onions quartered and flaked into
  individual 'petals'
sprinkling of marjoram
200g goats' cheese, chopped into small chunks

Leek, new potato & smoked Cheddar:
100g leeks, sliced and softened in a
  little butter
100g new potatoes, cubed and boiled
200g grated smoked Cheddar

Roasted red peppers & feta:
100g jarred roasted red peppers, cut into strips
200g feta, roughly crumbled

Courgette, lemon thyme & ricotta:
100g courgette, coarsely grated
  or finely chopped
sprinkling of lemon thyme
200g ricotta

RECIPE CONTINUED OVERLEAF

Preheat the oven to 180°C (160°C fan) and grease and flour a 28cm tart tin. This will give you a wide, shallow tart that looks great on the table. Use a narrower, taller tin if you need deeper, chunkier slices for picnic portability.

Remove the pastry from the fridge. If it's been in there a long time, i.e. overnight, get it out half an hour before so that it comes to room temperature. Lightly flour a surface and roll out the pastry until it's a few inches wider than the tin, Ensure it doesn't stick by moving it around gently as you work and keeping the surface well floured.

Roll the pastry over the rolling pin and then place it over the tart tin. Gently press into the sides, then trim the top edge all the way around with a sharp knife. Prick the base with a fork. Blind bake for 20 minutes until lightly golden – you don't want to overbake the edges, but nor do you want a soggy bottom.

Beat the eggs in a large jug, reserving a couple of tablespoons for egg washing.

After the 20 minutes of blind baking, paint the interior of the tart case with the egg wash and return to the oven for 5 minutes.

Reduce the oven temperature to 100°C (80°C fan).

Add the cream to the eggs, then season generously with salt and pepper. Mix well.

Arrange your chosen fillings in the tart case, then place it on the oven shelf. Carefully pour the custard mixture into the tart case to cover your filling, then close the oven door.

The longer and lower you can cook your custard, the smoother and more unctuous it will be. The core temperature of the custard needs to be 80°C to be perfectly and safely cooked, so any oven temperature of 100°C (80°C fan) or higher will eventually set it perfectly as long as you're not in a hurry.

There are two ways to be sure that your tart has a perfect texture. You can use the traditional 'wobble test' where you shake the tart gently and stop cooking when the custard 'wobbles' without 'slopping' but before it goes solid. It's a great trick, but you really need an experienced cook to show you how it's done. Rosie Sykes, our first chef at Fitzbillies, showed us her wobble in 2002 and our tarts have never been the same since. At home, we'd recommend doing the wobble test after 25 minutes of cooking time and at 10 minute intervals thereafter until set. You can also use a probe thermometer like our chefs, cooking in a low oven until the centre of the custard reaches 80°C.

If neither of these methods appeal, or if time is of the essence, cook at 200°C (180°C fan) for 45 minutes. This will give you a safe tart, though possibly a more rubbery one. Allow to cool before tucking in.

Cornish pasty

Everything in an artisan bakery is made by hand. Some things are made daily, some things are made in batches every few days and some get made and put on the menu as specials 'when we have time'. It is one of the great sadnesses of my life that we don't have the time to make Cornish pasties every day, but when we do, they are astonishing. Big, thick, generous and utterly fulfilling. We have a secret arrangement with the head waiters to text us whenever the pasties appear so that we can pop by for a 'quality-control spot check'.

The filling recipe is very specific, and although you can experiment, it's worth starting with this combination. Beef skirt is a cheap cut, full of flavour, that takes well to the steamy cooking inside the pasty case. The potato proportion gives a certain starchy body, the swede and carrot both bring sweetness and the onion all but renders into the juices of everything else. We strongly recommend you go crazy with the pepper too. Chopping up the meat and veg into small cubes sounds like a faff; but it's worth it so that everything will cook at the same rate.

Makes 10 pasties
325g beef skirt, cut into 1cm cubes
250g potatoes, peeled and cut
  into 1.5cm cubes
125g swede, peeled and cut into 1cm cubes
125g carrots, peeled and cut into 1cm cubes
100g onion, finely sliced
salt and ground white pepper
1kg shortcrust pastry (see recipe on page 159)
plain flour, for dusting

Preheat your oven to 200°C (180°C fan) and line a baking tray with baking parchment.

Combine the meat and veg in a bowl and season the mix liberally.

Remove the pastry from the fridge. If it's been in there a long time, i.e. overnight, get it out half an hour before so that it comes to room temperature. Divide the pastry into ten 100g balls and roll each out on a lightly floured surface into 15cm circles.

Divide the filling equally between the pastry circles, spooning a large mound into the centre of each circle. For those who enjoy precision, this will be 90g per pasty.

Paint a little water around the edge of the pastry circles, then pull over the pastry to enclose the filling and crimp the edges tightly together with your fingers.

Place your pasties on the lined baking tray and bake for 40 minutes. Allow to cool a little before diving in to eat – the filling is irresistible, but hotter than the surface of the sun.

The Fitzbillies year

The Fitzbillies year follows two calendars: the one followed by most of the Western world and the unique calendar of the University of Cambridge.

Alumni Weekend

The academic year of the University of Cambridge officially runs from 1 October to 30 September. The preceding weekend is Alumni Weekend and that's when it all really starts (and finishes) because former undergraduates of Cambridge colleges are invited back to the alma mater.

The superficial enticement is a programme of dinners and lectures put on by the colleges and university as part of their development programme (development in this case means fundraising). The real reason to return, as anyone who has ever loved and left an educational institution knows, is to meet up with old friends and revisit youthful haunts – including Fitzbillies.

It is perhaps our favourite weekend of the year. It is certainly when we learn the most about the history of Fitzbillies and shed the most tears over people's memories of their time in Cambridge and their visits to the shop.

Our favourite visitors are the octogenarians and nonagenarians who tell us their memories of Fitzbillies just after the war, when rationing was still in full force and through the 1950s and 60s. The food in colleges, as everywhere else, was in short supply and pretty dreadful. Fitzbillies Chelsea buns were one of the few delicious things you could still buy.

At the other end of the age range, people who were regular customers over the past few years and then one day simply vanished, graduating and going on to a new life, pop back to say hello and reminisce over a coffee and their favourite cake.

One of the things that has made Fitzbillies so beloved and so unusually famous for a small, regional cake shop is that, every year, a new cohort of undergraduates troops through our doors. Many visit regularly or come for special treats during three of the most formative years of their lives. Then they leave and travel all over the world, but they never forget their time in Cambridge or Fitzbillies.

October – term begins

The French have a word for it: *la rentrée*. We call it 'Back to College Weekend'. It usually starts on the Thursday or Friday before full term. The roads in the centre of Cambridge clog up with estate cars and four-wheel drives, piled to the roofs with the entire contents of student rooms. They have little choice but to pull up on the double yellows and throw their passengers out onto the pavement with everything from lacrosse sticks to ironing boards (yes, apparently undergraduates do iron). These are then transported around the streets and colleges to often distant rooms, on little hand barrows provided by the porters.

Then it's time for brunch, lunch or afternoon tea. And if you're at Pembroke, Peterhouse, St Catharine's or Corpus, about the closest place you could possibly go, to recover from the move and say goodbye to the parents, is Fitzbillies. So we brace ourselves for a day of excited 18-year-olds and wobbly-lipped parents. They seem to feel that Fitzbillies vouchers may save their offspring from starvation and that's fine by us.

Freshers' Week

If you stand in the queue in the coffee shop, you really know it's Freshers' Week. For the first few days, the talk is all: 'What did you get in your A Levels?'. For the next few days after that, the talk is all hangovers and the embarrassing antics of the night before. This will pass. It's just a phase.

It's easy to be cynical, and yes, our staff encounter their share of entitled and arrogant young people, but we love the enthusiasm, the hope, the energy of youngsters who have worked very hard to be here. Their excitement at starting on the next step of their journey to adult life is palpable. Good luck to them. They are going to have to work hard for their prized Cambridge degree.

Down to work

After the excitement of the start of term, reality sets in. For scientists, lectures, seminars, labs; for arts undergraduates, two essays a week, lectures, the library and supervisions. Fortunately, Fitzbillies is conveniently placed for the lecture halls in Mill Lane.

There is a bicycle rush hour each morning at five minutes to nine as everyone heads to their department or lecture hall. The queue in our coffee shops reaches its peak at this time as everyone realises they've left it just a bit too late to get a coffee and not be late for lectures.

Mid-morning, the café fills up with academics comparing notes from department meetings. And at lunchtime, students order grilled cheese toasties and professors entertain their lunch guests.

And so it continues for eight short weeks, then the parents are back to take the undergraduates home for Christmas. But no sooner do this year's crop become a term old than it's time for admissions interviews for next year's crop, and the café fills up again with nervous teenagers and their even more nervous parents.

Christmas

Term ends early in December, which means we can get down to some serious preparation for Christmas. We started making Christmas cakes and puddings in the quiet of September. Now we give the Christmas cakes their last drink of rum and put on the marzipan and icing.

The mince pie marathon begins. All the bakers, and as many other members of staff as are deemed competent, crowd around the giant tables in the bakery and, with the sort of production line that would make Henry Ford turn in his grave, produce thousands of the most delectable mince pies you will ever eat. They are often called 'Cambridge crack'.

There is no more encouraging sight than an entire bakery rack with every shelf loaded with Gill's mince pies. What continues to surprise us every year is how quickly they fly out of the shop. Same again tomorrow please.

January (and 'Veganuary')

Every business has a lean time. For us, it's the first three weeks of January. We understand that too much cake has consequences and that good things must be enjoyed in moderation.

Sales of smashed avocado on toast, always a popular option in the café, go through the roof. Cut the toast if you're low-carbing, and we have vegan cakes to get you through Veganuary. We find, though, that by Burns Night and the end of January pay-day weekend, most people are ready for a little of what they fancy and everyone in the cake world breathes a sigh of relief.

Valentine's Day

This usually coincides with the February half term, which makes it one of the busiest weeks of the year at Fitzbillies. It's too cold to be outdoors for long, so parents bring kids for a treat when they're out in town. Our hot chocolate, made with ganache from the bakery, is in high demand to revive weary families.

Red velvet cake seems to get more and more popular every year at Valentine's Day – perhaps it's the association between its blood-red colour and hearts. Boxes of macarons in beautiful pastel colours also fly out of the door.

Mother's Day

In the days running up to Mother's Day, our customers place their orders for Mother's Day lemon cakes, beautifully decorated with sugar daffodils, or pick up a box of macarons or an afternoon tea token as a gift.

On the Sunday itself, the café fills with big family tables for brunch or afternoon tea. There is something marvellously multi-generational about a bakery. Where can you take your great-grandmother, your teenager and your toddler? Not to a pub, not to a fine-dining restaurant. You can take them all to Fitzbillies and people regularly do.

Easter

We wish Easter would stay still. The way it moves around makes it really hard to plan properly in the bakery. Sometimes it coincides with the end of one term, sometimes with the beginning of the next. If anyone in the Vatican is reading this, please can you sort it out?

The big question at Fitzbillies is when to start making hot cross buns. It feels like customers begin asking for them as soon as Christmas is over, but we like to keep them special and start making them just a couple of weeks before Easter. Our regular customers make a special journey as soon as they know they are in.

Simnel cake is the other important Easter tradition. A light fruit cake with a layer of marzipan baked in the middle with another on top. And 11 round balls of marzipan to decorate: one for each of the disciples, except Judas, for obvious reasons.

Summer term

There is no more beautiful place on earth than Cambridge in May and June. When the weather is fine, we get as close to café society as you are ever going to get in the Fens. Pimm's and prosecco become acceptable a little earlier in the day and Fitzbillies stays open longer in the evening as we attempt an East Anglian version of the *passeggiata*.

The sheer volume of lush greenery and waves of cow parsley in the meadows tempt everyone out of doors. The demand for picnics, from the simple takeaway sandwich to the grand wicker-hamper affair, increases. And if it's too hot for Chelsea buns, there is always Chelsea bun ice cream. Our Bridge Street branch fills with groups, stocking up before they go on a punt trip or taking their purchases to enjoy on the grass at the Mill Pond or Jesus Green.

It's a wonderful and brutal time to be an undergraduate, especially a Finalist. Enjoy your last summer in Cambridge or get your head down and do some work in the library…

Wedding-cake season

From Easter until September we make at least one or two wedding cakes each weekend. On the busiest weekends we can make up to four wedding cakes, but never more, so that we can be sure each gets the special attention it deserves. We suspect Cambridge has more than its fair share of weddings, as so many former undergraduates come back to get married in their old colleges.

The life cycle of a wedding cake usually starts about six months before the wedding – the previous autumn for spring weddings, January for later summer weddings. We have a consultation with the bride and groom, which is an excuse to taste lots of cakes, establish their favourite flavours and discuss styles, colours and flower arrangements.

Wedding cakes, of course, have changed a huge amount in the last hundred years. We could write a book about that alone (perhaps we will). For the first half of Fitzbillies' 100-year history, there were only royal-iced fruit cakes (unless you count the cardboard constructions with a tiny fruit cake hidden inside that had to make do during the war). Then in the 1980s and '90s the introduction of rolled sugarpaste icing meant couples could have sponge cakes rather than fruit cakes. More recently, we shifted to making mainly naked or semi-naked sponge cakes, beautifully decorated with fresh fruit and flowers. Much nicer to eat than slabs of fondant icing.

We sometimes think the most difficult part of the wedding-cake business is actually delivering the cakes in central Cambridge. Saturday mornings see us running the gauntlet of parties of tourists, predatory traffic wardens and random road closures to get giant, heavy, fragile cakes over cobbles, through courtyards and into upstairs halls. We're always relieved and delighted when the cake is in place, on its stand. It's a great privilege to contribute to such an important day and we secretly like to have a good look inside the most beautiful rooms in the colleges.

June–May Week

Fans of Clive James, a long-time resident of Cambridge, will be well aware that May Week is in June. It combines the May Bumps (the peak of the rowing year, after the Boat Race, of course) with garden parties, May Balls and other parties (known as 'Events' or 'Affairs' to make them seem less grand).

In the Fitzbillies bakery, we produce thousands of mini cakes for these college events: mini canapé-sized scones pre-filled with jam and cream, mini fruit tarts and éclairs. And the Fitzbillies classic, now only made to order, the fondant fancy (page 89). They have little in common with the Mr Kipling's variety, but their old-fashioned pastel beauty adds a touch of nostalgia to any tea party.

General Admissions

The natural culmination of the academic year is General Admissions, otherwise known as Degree Days. All the students graduating that year are 'admitted' to the degree of Bachelor of Arts or Science (or various other ranks). This happens over four days at the end of June. The members of each college who are taking their degrees walk in procession, in full academic dress (gowns and mortarboards), to the Senate House, led by the dignitaries of their college.

We love watching the processions. It's a great piece of theatre that marks the end of three years of hard work and achievement (in most cases). And of course, once the ceremony is over, it's all back to Fitzbillies for tea. It's a proud moment for the parents and the end to a journey that often began with them visiting Cambridge (and Fitzbillies) for open days and interviews four years earlier.

And just when we think it's all over, the University of Cambridge keeps on giving. For three days in early July the town is awash with sixth-formers, visiting colleges and departments on Open Days as they work out their preferred home for their degree. They are all hungry, they are all in a hurry. They all want a Fitzbillies Chelsea bun and a sandwich with a very plain filling.

The Long Vac

After the high jinks of May Week and General Admissions, the summer used to be a quiet period in Cambridge. That was before cultural tourism became what it is today.

Throughout the summer, a constant flow of language-school students and tour groups of all nationalities streams through Cambridge. For the local businesses it's mainly a blessing, but for many of the locals it's an irritation. You certainly don't want to try cycling along King's Parade on a Saturday in July.

We're very lucky that Fitzbillies is high up there on the list of 'What to do in Cambridge'. For some, it's all about sampling the famous Chelsea buns. For others, it's the English afternoon tea. So, for most of the summer it's three-tiered cake stands, finger sandwiches and Google translate at the ready to welcome our visitors.

September

And now we can take a breath. The tourists have gone. The academic year hasn't restarted. The kids are back in school. All is calm. September is the month that Cambridge belongs to the people of Cambridge.

Early autumn is a time of beautiful clear days, the 'Open Cambridge' weekend and the 'Bridge the Gap' annual charity walk for the Arthur Rank Hospice. If you want to walk around the city or persuade the porters to let you look around one of the colleges, now is your time. There are also no queues for punts.

Fitzbillies starts to refill with regular faces, back from their summer holidays. Groups of parents who have dropped the kids back to school and want to catch up; freelance workers furiously answering emails and typing documents on their laptops; local office workers combining a meeting with a crafty bun in the café; Saturday shoppers wanting a break from the shops of the Grand Arcade.

Make the most of the quiet while it lasts because the inexorable rhythm of Cambridge life goes on – and it's all about to start again.

SEASONAL SPECIALS

It doesn't take an anthropologist to spot that cake has an important role to play in most of our celebrations and has done so (in one form or another) since the earliest times. In the bakery we find there is always something to celebrate, whether it's the traditional festivals of Christmas, Mother's Day and Easter or the ever-more popular Valentine's Day and Halloween. The first batches of hot cross buns and mince pies never fail to delight us. And if there's nothing particular in the calendar, we make our own celebration of the fantastic local, seasonal fruit from East Anglia and beyond.

Seasonal fruit upside-down cakes

*This cake will take you through every season.
They all look beautiful and taste amazing.*

For the cake mixture
*200g unsalted butter, softened,
    plus extra for greasing*
200g caster sugar
200g self-raising flour
1½ tsp baking powder
2 tsp vanilla paste
3 medium eggs
60ml full-fat milk

Spring – Rhubarb
100g unsalted butter
100g caster sugar
1kg pink rhubarb, cut into 10cm lengths

Summer – Nectarine & raspberry
100g unsalted butter
100g caster sugar
4 nectarines, sliced
100g fresh raspberries

Autumn – Pear & ginger
100g unsalted butter
100g caster sugar
60g crystallised ginger, chopped
5 pears, peeled, cored and sliced
2 tsp ground ginger, to add to the cake mix

Winter – Blood orange
210g caster sugar
100ml water
*4 blood oranges, skin on, sliced
    and pips removed*

Preheat the oven to 190°C (170°C fan). Grease and line a deep 25cm cake tin.

If you are making the spring or summer cake, gently melt the butter and sugar together in a small saucepan, then pour this into the bottom of the tin. Arrange your chosen fruit on top.

If you are making the autumn cake, melt the butter, sugar and crystallised ginger together in a small saucepan, then pour this into the bottom of the tin. Arrange the pears on top.

If you are making the winter cake, heat the sugar and water in a pan until nearly boiling. Add the sliced oranges and simmer for 10 minutes. Remove the orange slices and put aside to cool, then continue to boil the syrup until it thickens slightly. Pour the syrup into the base of the tin and arrange the oranges on top.

Now make up your cake mixture. Place all the ingredients into the bowl of a stand mixer and beat for 5 minutes until pale and fluffy. If making the autumn cake, add the ground ginger.

Spoon the batter on top of the prepared fruit in the bottom of the tin and level with a spatula.

Bake for 35 minutes until golden and the cake springs back to the touch. Leave to cool in the tin for 10 minutes, then turn the cake out upside down onto a plate. It is important to turn it out before the cake is cool.

Hot cross buns

Hot cross buns are an Easter tradition. Originally they were made only on Maundy Thursday, the day before Good Friday. In the days before they could be bought from supermarkets, the bakers at Fitzbillies worked a double shift to make enough and there were queues round the block.

Makes 16 buns
610g strong white flour, plus extra for dusting
40g unsalted butter or baking margarine, softened
40g caster sugar
¼ tsp salt
1 medium egg
7g fast-action dried yeast
1½ tsp mixed spice
170g currants
115g sultanas
30g mixed candied peel
100–150ml hand-hot water, around 37°C

For the piping paste
4 tbsp plain flour
4 tbsp caster sugar
1 tsp sunflower oil
1–2 tbsp cold water

For the glaze
100g caster sugar
50ml water

Put the flour, butter or margarine, caster sugar, salt, egg, yeast, mixed spice and 100ml of the hand-hot water into the bowl of a stand mixer fitted with the dough hook. Mix on medium speed for 8 minutes to make a very soft, smooth dough. (If the dough seems too stiff, add the extra 50ml of water.) Add the currants, sultanas and mixed peel and mix for another minute.

Turn the dough out onto a lightly floured surface and knead quickly into a ball. Place the dough into a clean bowl, cover with cling film and prove in a warm place for 1 hour or until doubled in size.

Turn the dough out onto a lightly floured work surface and gently press out into a rectangle to deflate. Divide the dough into 16 pieces and shape each piece into a neat ball.

Line a large baking tray with baking parchment and arrange the balls of dough in straight lines four by four with gaps between them so that when the buns have doubled in size they will just touch. Cover with a damp tea towel and leave in a warm place for 45 minutes, or until the buns have doubled in size.

Preheat the oven to 190°C (170°C fan).

Make the piping paste by mixing together all the ingredients, then put in a piping bag with a small plain nozzle. (Or use a plastic freezer bag with the corner cut off.) Pipe a cross onto each bun.

Bake the buns for 30–40 minutes until they are golden and sound hollow when tapped on the base.

To make the glaze, put the sugar and water in a pan and bring to the boil. Brush the hot glaze over the buns.

Simnel cake

Simnel cake is a very old recipe, traditionally made for both Mother's Day and Easter, and characteristically has a layer of marzipan baked into the middle of the cake. Customers come in weeks before Easter to check we will be making simnel cake that year, when it will be available and whether they can place an order.

1 batch of marzipan (see recipe on page 187),
    or 500g ready-made marzipan
135g caster sugar, plus extra for dusting
60g unsalted butter, softened, plus extra
    for greasing
60g baking margarine, softened
3 medium eggs
180g self-raising flour
90ml full-fat milk
100g currants
100g sultanas
30g apricot jam, strained

Make the marzipan according to the recipe on page 187, ideally the day before you bake so that it has time to chill overnight (a couple of hours in the fridge is also fine).

Preheat the oven to 170°C (150°C fan). Grease and line a deep 18cm cake tin (usually 8cm deep).

Cream the sugar, butter and margarine together in a stand mixer until pale and fluffy. Then add the eggs, one at a time, beating well between each addition.

Sift in the flour and mix, making sure to scrape down the sides of the bowl. With the mixer still running, slowly pour in the milk. Add the currants and sultanas and mix until just combined.

Spoon half the cake mixture into the tin and level it gently with a spatula.

Take 200g of the marzipan, or ready-made marzipan, and roll it into a ball. On a surface lightly dusted with caster sugar, roll the marzipan ball out into a circle the size of your cake tin. Place the marzipan on top of the cake mixture in the tin.

Put the rest of the cake mixture into the tin and level it gently with a spatula.

Bake for 35–40 minutes until the cake is golden on the top.

Leave the cake in the tin to cool completely.

RECIPE CONTINUED OVERLEAF

When the cake is cool, take 110g of the remaining marzipan and roll it into eleven 10g balls. Put them to one side for a moment.

Lightly dust a surface with caster sugar and roll the remaining marzipan into a ball, then into a thick circle the size of the cake.

Put the apricot jam in a small saucepan and bring it to the boil. Brush the jam all over the top of the cake, reserving a little to stick the balls on.

Place the marzipan on top of the cake and press down gently. Press the edges in so that it fits the top of the cake seamlessly.

Dip the base of each marzipan ball into a little warm apricot jam, to act as glue, and place them evenly around the top of the cake.

Finally, if you have one, blowtorch the top of the cake to toast the marzipan a little and get a nice brown colour on the centre of the cake and the tops of each 'disciple'. Untoasted marzipan will also look fine.

Marzipan

Homemade marzipan is delicious and this type is very simple to make. It makes enough for a simnel cake or Christmas cake.

Makes 500g
250g ground almonds
250g icing sugar, plus a little extra if needed
juice of ½ lemon
2 medium egg yolks, lightly beaten, plus
    a little extra if needed

Mix the ground almonds and icing sugar together in a bowl.

Add the lemon juice and egg yolks and mix to combine. You want a nice soft dough texture so that you can roll the marzipan out without it cracking. If it's a bit dry, add a little more egg yolk. If it's a bit soft, add a little bit more icing sugar.

Roll into a ball, wrap in cling film and chill in the fridge for a few hours or ideally overnight.

Meringue ghosts

When running a bakery, you tend to use a lot of egg yolks, which in turn leaves you with a lot of egg whites as a by-product. Instead of letting them go to waste we make meringues to use them all up. By an interesting supernatural coincidence, meringue ghosts were first reported by the bakers soon after we took over. They tend to manifest in the bakery in the weeks leading up to Halloween and, far from being in any way scary, are actually jolly little things and very popular with small people.

Though they disappear in November, their close relatives, meringue snowmen (see photo on page 193), appear in the shop in December, just in time for Christmas.

240g egg whites (240g is roughly the whites of 6 medium eggs)
420g caster sugar
400g 54% dark chocolate

(If making the snowmen, you will also need coloured royal icing to pipe their faces and scarves.)

Preheat the oven to 120°C (100°C fan).
Line a baking tray with baking parchment.

In a very clean bowl of a stand mixer, whisk the egg whites until frothy.

Keep the mixer on maximum speed and add the caster sugar, a teaspoon at a time. Continue to whisk until mixture is stiff and shiny.

Transfer the mixture to a piping bag (or a plastic freezer bag with the corner snipped off) and begin piping your ghosts onto the lined baking tray. Ghosts are fickle creatures and will simply flop from boredom if left standing around. It's almost impossible to describe the shape a ghost should be, perhaps because they are made of ectoplasm or perhaps because they are entirely imaginary, but use the picture here as a guide.

Bake your ghosts for 1 hour 10 minutes.

You can tell when a ghost is done by lifting it off the baking parchment and tapping its bottom. If it's done, it will sound hollow… or say 'Whooooooooooo!'

Melt the chocolate in the microwave (give it 20 seconds on medium and stir, then another 20 seconds until melted), or in a heatproof bowl set over a pan of barely simmering water. Dip the ghosts' bottoms into the melted chocolate to form a neat little base, then lay the ghosts on their sides while their bottoms set. Use the remaining chocolate in a small piping bag to pipe on eyes.

Christmas cake

This cake should be made at least a month before Christmas so that there is plenty of time to feed it with rum, but you can start even earlier than that – the cake gets more delicious as it matures. We often start making the Christmas cakes in September.

120g chopped glacé cherries
350g currants
450g sultanas
zest and juice of 1 lemon
zest and juice of 1 orange
100ml rum, plus extra to feed the cake
*   and for icing*
250g light brown soft sugar
250g unsalted butter, softened,
*   plus extra for greasing*
1 tbsp black treacle
250g plain flour
½ tsp ground cinnamon
¼ tsp mixed spice
¼ tsp salt
3 medium eggs

For the icing
1 batch of marzipan (see recipe on page 187),
*   or 500g ready-made marzipan*
icing sugar, for dusting
150g apricot jam, strained and boiled
500g ready-to-roll white fondant icing
500g royal icing sugar, for piping decorations

Mix together the cherries, dried fruit, lemon and orange zest and juice and the rum in a bowl, cover and leave to soak overnight.

The next day, preheat the oven to 180°C (160°C fan). Grease and line a 20cm cake tin. Fold a piece of brown paper or newspaper so that it is four layers thick and long enough to wrap around the tin. Tie it around the tin with string. This will stop the outside of the cake overbaking and burning.

Cream the brown sugar, butter and treacle in a stand mixer until pale and fluffy. Then mix the flour, cinnamon, mixed spice and salt together in another bowl. Add the eggs to the creamed mixture, one at a time, mixing in a little of the flour mixture after each addition. When all the eggs are in, add the remaining flour and mix gently. Tip in the fruit mixture and stir again until just combined.

Tip the mixture into the prepared tin and smooth the top with a spatula. Bake for 2¼ hours until a skewer inserted into the middle comes out clean. Let the cake cool completely in the tin.

The next day, take the cake out of the tin, poke holes in it with a skewer and pour over a couple of tablespoons of rum. Then wrap the cake in cling film and store in a tin. Repeat weekly for 4 weeks (or more if you're keen on booze). The cake is now ready to be marzipan-ed.

RECIPE CONTINUED OVERLEAF

Make a batch of marzipan according to the recipe on page 187 or use ready-made marzipan. Homemade marzipan tastes extra delicious, but has raw egg in it, so if you are making for anyone in an at-risk group (e.g. pregnant, elderly), it may be better to use shop-bought.

Split the marzipan into two balls, using one third of the mixture to make one ball and two thirds to make the second. Measure the circumference of the cake and the height from top to bottom.

Roll the larger ball of marzipan into a long sausage, nearly as long as the measurement you took for the circumference – it will grow a bit more as you roll it. Put the sausage on a work surface that is lightly dusted with icing sugar and use a rolling pin to widen and flatten it until it has reached the height of the cake. Trim it a bit or pat it into shape as necessary.

Brush the sides of the cake with the apricot jam, then wrap the strip of marzipan around it, making sure the ends meet and the entire side of the cake is covered. Tease the marzipan into shape – pulling, patting, cutting and trimming are legitimate methods – then roll the pin around it to help get it smooth.

Now measure the diameter of the cake, including the marzipan. Take the smaller ball of marzipan and roll it out, moving it round on the board and rolling in different directions to keep it circular. Keep patting it back into shape. Once it's the size of the cake, paint the top of the cake with apricot jam. Turn the cake upside down onto the circle of marzipan and use a palette knife to push in the edges of the marzipan to create a neat edge and join the marzipan round the sides. Flip the cake back over and leave the marzipan to dry out for a day before adding the icing.

The next day, roll out the fondant icing into a smooth ball on a very clean work surface lightly dusted with icing sugar. Measure right over the cake from the bottom of one side, over the top and to the bottom of the other side and roll the icing into a circle to match. Keep the work surface dusted with icing sugar and keep moving the icing so that it doesn't stick.

Brush the cake with rum to act as glue so that the icing will adhere to the marzipan. Roll the icing circle gently over the rolling pin to lift it and then place it over the cake. Use the palms of your hands (not your fingers) to very gently smooth it down. Trim the excess round the bottom. If the bottom looks a bit messy, don't worry, you can put a ribbon round it.

Now decorate your cake. We pipe on decorations using royal icing sugar (make up according to the instructions on the packet), as we think it looks prettiest and you don't see it on mass-produced cakes. You could use shapes cut out from more rolled icing – stars, snowflakes or Christmas trees. Or you could use ornaments – we love the vintage plaster Santas and snowmen. You could, of course, royal ice your cake. Until a few years ago that's what we did. But more and more customers did not like the traditional hard icing, so we succumbed and went for fondant icing.

Decorated Genoa cake

This is the recipe that Fitzbillies has always given out whenever it's been asked to contribute a recipe to a cookbook. It is the recipe included in Jane Grigson's Observer Guide to British Cookery, *first published in 1984. We still make it at Christmas for those people (and there are some) who prefer their fruit cake without marzipan and icing. We always love its beautiful, jewel-like topping.*

> *150g caster sugar*
> *150g salted butter, softened*
> *3 medium eggs, at room temperature*
> *175g plain flour*
> *150g currants*
> *150g sultanas*
> *40g golden syrup*
> *125g glacé cherries*
> *75g blanched almonds*
> *75g pecans*

Preheat the oven to 200°C (180°C fan) and line an 18cm round cake tin with baking parchment so that it comes 2.5cm above the rim.

Cream together the caster sugar and butter in a stand mixer until pale and fluffy. Beat in the eggs, one at a time, then stir in half the flour.

Mix the other half of the flour with the currants and sultanas, then carefully fold this into the rest of the mixture.

Pour the batter into the prepared cake tin and bake for 15 minutes, then lower the heat to 190°C (170°C fan) and bake for a further 30 minutes until the cake is lightly golden and just springs back to the touch. If the cake is starting to brown too much, cover the top with a double thickness of baking parchment.

Meanwhile, make the topping. In a saucepan, warm the golden syrup slightly to make it more runny, then gently mix in the glacé cherries, almonds and pecans.

When the cake comes out of the oven, spread this topping over the top of the cake and press it down evenly with wet fingers. Then place it back in the oven for a further 20 minutes until lightly browned.

Leave to cool completely in the tin.

Mince pies

Every year we wonder how early to start making mince pies. We try to hold off because we don't like the way Christmas seems to get earlier every year, but by early December we usually succumb to demand and the first mince pies appear in the shop. Our mince pies have a lot of fans. It's the pastry that makes them really special – almost like shortbread. One is never enough.

Makes 24 pies
240g self-raising flour, plus extra for dusting
40g caster sugar, plus extra for sprinkling
115g unsalted butter, cold and cubed, plus
    extra for greasing
100g baking margarine, cold and cubed
1 medium egg, beaten
1 tbsp cold water, plus extra if needed

For the mincemeat (If you don't want to make
    mincemeat, use a 1kg jar or two 410g jars
    of high-quality, shop-bought mincemeat)
100g currants
100g raisins
100g sultanas
100g Bramley apple, peeled, cored and
    chopped into small pieces
50g mixed candied peel
100g dark muscovado sugar
50g vegetable suet
½ tsp mixed spice
zest and juice of 1 lemon
zest and juice of 1 orange

If you are making your own mincemeat, start the day before you want to make the pies (or up to a week before) and mix together all the ingredients. Keep in the fridge until you need it.

Preheat the oven to 180°C (160°C fan) and grease and flour two jam tart trays (most are for 12 tarts), unless yours are non-stick.

Put the flour and sugar into a large bowl and add the butter and margarine. Rub it in with your fingertips. Add the beaten egg and cold water and bring the pastry together gently. Add a little bit more water if necessary. Wrap and refrigerate the pastry for 1 hour.

Roll half the pastry out on a floured work surface to a thickness of 5mm. Cut out 24 rounds using a 6mm cutter – these are for the tops. You cut the tops first because if the pastry starts to get tougher with repeat rolling, it will be less noticeable on the bottom.

Take the remaining pastry and roll it out a little thinner than previously – 4mm thick. Cut out 24 circles with a 7mm cutter and press these gently into the indentations of the jam tart tins.

Put a heaped tablespoon of mincemeat into each tart and place a lid on top, sealing lightly together. Lightly sprinkle with sugar. Bake for 25–30 minutes until light golden in colour.

Leave to cool, then remove from the tin after half an hour or so. Sprinkle a little more sugar on the top if you wish.

Gingerbread

We always make gingerbread at Christmas: Gingerbread people so as to delight children and beautifully decorated gingerbread for Christmas tree decorations, with a hole to thread a ribbon and hang on the tree. They tend not to survive on the tree for long in houses where there are children (or dogs). How many you make will depend on the size of your cutters.

170g caster sugar
100g unsalted butter, softened
70g baking margarine, softened
200g golden syrup
400g plain flour, plus extra for dusting
1 tbsp bicarbonate of soda
1 ½ tbsp ground ginger
½ tsp mixed spice

For the decoration
250g or about ½ pack royal icing sugar
(one that already includes powdered
egg white, so that all you have to do is
add water)

Preheat the oven to 180°C (160°C fan) and line as many baking trays as you happen to have with baking parchment.

Cream the caster sugar, butter and margarine together in a bowl until just combined and then beat in the golden syrup.

In another bowl, combine the flour, bicarbonate of soda, ginger and mixed spice, then stir into the creamed mixture to form a dough. Don't overmix, otherwise the biscuits will be tough.

Wrap the dough in cling film and chill for 1 hour in the fridge.

Remove from the fridge and roll out the dough on a lightly floured surface to a thickness of 6mm.

Cut out gingerbread people, houses, stars or any shape of your choice. If you would like to use them as Christmas tree decorations, use the end of a drinking straw to cut a small hole, not too close to the edge, so that you can thread a ribbon through.

Place on the lined baking trays and bake in the oven for 25–30 minutes. The biscuits will rise up and then collapse – at this stage they should be ready.

Remove from oven, leave them on the tray for a few minutes and then transfer to a cooling rack.

Once the biscuits are completely cool, you are ready to decorate. Make up the royal icing sugar according to the packet instructions. You will need an electric mixer or whisk for this.

Fit a piping bag with a No. 2 straight writing nozzle and fill it with icing – don't overfill it or it will all squirt out the back onto your hands. (Or use a plastic freezer bag with the corner cut off.)

Pipe a mouth, nose, eyes and buttons onto your gingerbread people and any design of your choice onto your other shapes. Leave to set for a few moments before nibbling.

HEAD BAKER (BREAD): PAUL WHITE

Paul White is the most recent addition to the Fitzbillies family. We had not made our own bread for many years, so, when one of our best suppliers was struck by illness, we quickly decided to buy his bread bakery. We then desperately needed a head baker. There were plenty of people interested (bread baking is a pretty cool thing to be involved in at the moment), but Paul stood head and shoulders above all the others.

When he left school in London, Paul began training as a chef but very quickly moved to a small traditional bakery in the Midlands. This was back in the days before bread making was a fashionable pursuit for tattooed young gentlemen, so it was an unusual choice, but it resulted in a very traditional training in the mechanics of a small town's bakery, together with the age-old skills of an artisan.

For a while, Paul held a job that sounds about as much like the SAS as you can get in the world of cottage loaves and brioche buns. He joined a large chain bakery as a 'relief baker' and troubleshooter. Because his skills were so comprehensive and he was so adaptable in personality, he travelled all over the country, covering shifts for craft bakers behind busy bread and cake shops. He tells hair-raising tales of finishing a shift, driving across the country and starting another within hours. It was punishing, but it left him with an ability to produce brilliant bread under almost any circumstances. There is no culture that will die on him, no exploding oven at 4am that will stop him filling the delivery baskets. No normal human can put up with that level of work pressure forever, so Paul moved to be the number two baker at the famous craft bakery at Hambleton Hall, teaching bread-making at diploma level.

FANCY BREADS

Our bakery today is a purpose-designed, highly organised space fitted with the best equipment to improve the quality of our baking and the working lives of the staff. It's hard to imagine what the first bakers would have made of computerised rotating ovens, temperature-controlled water supplies, laser thermometers and fermenting chambers. During the day shift, the bakers make the cakes that Fitzbillies has always been most famous for, but at night the bread bakers take over. We could write a whole book about their work… in fact, we probably will, but here we'll just cover some of the 'fancy breads' that are the biggest part of the Fitzbillies story.

There are some adaptations within this chapter for domestic kitchens, but the results will be the same. Water in the recipes should be pleasantly warm – imagine bathwater for a baby. We've specified 'dried active yeast', which is the easiest to find in the supermarket and comes in useful 7g envelopes. In the bakery we use fresh yeast. It's lovely, rich-smelling, creamy stuff that looks like loaves of caramel. Until very recently it was the law in this country that a baker would have to provide fresh yeast to anyone who asked for it. Though it's no longer a legal requirement, we, like most bakers, are still happy to give it out – it feels good to encourage the kind of cooking we all love. Even supermarket bakeries can usually be persuaded to hand over a little if asked nicely. If you can get your hands on the fresh stuff, just add double the quantity the recipe gives for the dried stuff. Yeast doesn't like salt, so, when pouring your dry ingredients into the mixing bowl, keep the yeast and the salt well apart at first.

When baking at any kind of batch size, the freezer is your friend. Many savoury goods, bread included, can be deep-frozen at various points in the process, so you can start again later with no loss of quality. It's particularly true of good bread.

The biggest difference between home and professional bakers' ovens is the facility to steam, which has several positive effects on the crust.

- Steam 'gelatinises' the starches in the crust, basically turning the starch into a shiny gel that sets into a hard but thin, shiny crust.

- It keeps the crust soft for the first stage, allowing for 'oven spring'.

It is possible to get a good steaming effect in most domestic ovens. Place a metal roasting tin on the floor of your electric oven, then preheat the oven at maximum temperature early. Half-fill a tea cup with cool water, then when your bread is ready to bake and your oven is at maximum heat, turn it off completely. Immediately load your bread into oven, then quickly but carefully pour the water into the hot roasting tray. This will sizzle and steam. Close the door of the oven and set a timer for 5 minutes for rolls or 7 minutes for bread. Start the timer as you close the door, and when the timer goes off, turn your oven back on.

For gas ovens, mist the bread with a conventional water spray bottle and bake without turning the oven off at all.

Soda bread

Regular bread comes from the bakery, but our soda bread, always amazingly popular with lunchtime customers, is made by the chefs. Most bring their own recipe or will have very strong opinions about 'upgrading' our previous recipe. But Chef Dan Peirce's recipe lingered long in the memory of staff and customers alike. It's dark with an almost smoky quality to it, and although we will probably go to hell for admitting it, it's even better with cream cheese and salmon than a bagel.

Makes 4 small loaves
500g plain flour
215g wholemeal flour
215g Granary flour
50g white granulated sugar
20g bicarbonate of soda
7.5g cream of tartar
1 litre buttermilk
75g honey
125g unsalted butter, melted
2 medium eggs, beaten
mix of seeds (we use a roughly equal quantity
    of pumpkin, poppy, sunflower and linseed)
    or rolled oats, for sprinkling

Soda bread dough starts 'working' as soon as the wet ingredients are added and there isn't much time to be getting things ready, so preheat your oven to 210°C (190°C fan) and line four 500g loaf tins with baking parchment.

Combine all the dry ingredients (except the seed mix) in a large mixing bowl.

Combine the wet ingredients in another bowl, then add to the dry ingredients and work by hand until the mixture is smooth and roughly the consistency of a Victoria sponge batter. Try not to overwork the ingredients, as this will overdevelop the gluten and make for a denser loaf.

Divide the dough evenly between the loaf tins. Sprinkle the tops with a seed mix or rolled oats.

Cover with foil and bake for 20 minutes, then reduce the oven temperature to 190°C (170°C fan), uncover and bake for another 20 minutes. The finished loaf has a cake-like consistency, so you can check that it's done when a skewer inserted into the middle comes out clean.

Brioche or hot dog rolls

Brioche is a fancy bread enriched with eggs and butter. The French love it for breakfast with a coffee, but we Brits seem to have taken to it as the ideal bun for a burger or a hot dog – maybe it's how well the soft, sweet crumb works with the salty meat. When the barbecues come out for a hot Cambridge weekend, we can scarcely bake enough of these.

We probably won't be putting anything as fashionable as a hot dog on the menu at Fitzbillies any time soon, but whenever the bakery does a batch of these, the chefs will make themselves one of our in-house secrets. Take two of our custom-made sausages, untwist the link between them and squeeze the filling until you have one single, double-length banger. Grill to perfection, then sling into a warm brioche roll, and cover with our fruit ketchup and English mustard.

Makes 10 buns
135ml hand-hot water, around 37°C
50g unsalted butter, softened
3 medium eggs, plus 2 eggs for egg washing
300g strong white flour
300g plain flour
35g caster sugar
14g salt
25g dried active yeast

Add the water, butter and eggs to the bowl of a stand mixer, then add all the other ingredients (except for the two eggs for egg washing). The yeast and the salt should be placed on different sides of the bowl.

Mix with a dough hook on the slow setting for 8 minutes, scraping down the sides occasionally. Now turn your mixer up to a moderate speed and mix for 6 minutes, or until dough is even in colour and texture and has a slight shine. Leave for 40 minutes at room temperature in the mixing bowl with a damp tea towel covering the top (this is called the bulk fermentation stage).

Tip the dough onto a clean surface (you will not need to add flour to the surface, as the fats in the butter and eggs make the dough easy to manage) and knead fairly vigorously for a few minutes, knocking the gases out of the dough to even out the bubbles and help further develop the dough's strength (this is called knocking back).

Once knocked back, divide the dough into ten 100g balls. Shape the pieces into round balls for buns or sausage shapes for hot dog rolls. Place onto two trays lined with baking parchment, leaving room for the rolls to grow.

Now beat together the remaining two eggs and brush generously over the buns.

Leave the buns in a warm room away from any draughts until nearly doubled in size – this should take 35–50 minutes. Preheat the oven to 230°C (210°C fan).

When doubled in size, spray the rolls with a misting of water and bake for 12–15 minutes until they have become a shiny chestnut brown.

The Fitzbillies bacon roll

From the very first days of menu planning, one thing was apparent: we could have excellent cakes, great buns and outstanding cups of quality coffee, but Fitzbillies, a café in a university town, would fail without a world-class bacon roll.

It sounds like such a simple thing, doesn't it? A roll, a fried rasher or two, a selection of sauces and Bob's your uncle… but that would be missing the point. People hold extremely strong opinions on bacon rolls – and by 'people' we mean everyone in the country who's not a vegetarian – so woe betide the business that serves an average one. You don't need 100 branches nationally, a research kitchen and a highly trained kitchen brigade to make a good one – and that's the problem. Big and established businesses have no inherent advantage in any bacon roll competition because anyone with sufficient passion, love, care and attention to detail can compete. So ours would have to be the best.

Surprisingly, the bacon is not actually the most difficult component. Some people like streaky, some lean, some like smoked, some unsmoked, but all can be satisfied with a decent, quality commercial rasher. Artisanal bacons are second to none in the unforgiving arena of the fry-up, but, like a really fulfilling burger, you can waste a lot of money and energy on very premium meat, only to discover that the more consistent, sustainable but mass-market versions are what the public wants.

The silent partner

No, the really key ingredient is the bun. As is the way in Cambridge, for months before we placed rasher in roll, we debated it theoretically in Jesuitical detail. It must be white – dietary fibre was never going to be part of the appeal. It must have a soft crust, preferably dusted with flour that gets all over your fingers and beard. It should have a soft, regular crumb, strong enough to stand up to any bacon grease and the customer's sauce-load. We felt the bread should be oval, so it could be well packed with long rashers without the grill man having to cut or bend pieces to fit. Al felt it should take butter.

Baking the roll fell to our favourite local baker, Alan Ackroyd. As a young man he'd trained at Fitzbillies and now ran Cambridge Organic Bakery, a small operation on the edge of town turning out astonishing breads with organic ingredients and absolutely no additives. It was Alan who remembered a particular soft white roll from the old 1958 menu that, back in the day, was considered a classier, more refined bread.

It was a shoo-in for our requirements, and within days, we were shovelling bacon into big, soft, pillowy baps and testing them on the staff. Alan continued to make the rolls for Fitzbillies right up until 2018 when he suddenly fell ill. We couldn't face the possibility of losing the world's best roll and so it seemed the happiest result for all of us to buy the bakery ourselves and continue to run it with the same staff, the same recipes and with Alan's blessing. Today the bakery is run by Paul White (page 201) who has also brought us his incredible skills with sourdough. The bacon roll, though, remains exactly the same and always will.

Assembling our roll

To keep them at their peak, the rolls are split just before the sandwich is made. They are buttered, liberally, and then placed face down on the griddle, just enough to get the lightest of tans.

The bacon is laid on, a little hanging over at each end, and for those that believe the Mona Lisa would be improved by fairy lights and a pink feather boa, we can add an egg. We let the customer choose the sauce. Of course, the sensible ones choose brown sauce, but as we've aged, we've grown more tolerant of the other choice – it's probably what they prefer in Oxford…

Floury white baps

This is the famous soft roll devised for the bacon bap. There is absolutely nothing unusual in the ingredients – it's pretty much the simplest dough you can make, but judging the cooking time perfectly makes the texture immensely pleasing and the simplicity means you can taste the quality of the excellent flour we get from a local mill.

It's a strange thing, but the results are almost creamy – so much so that other bakers won't believe we're not adding milk to the mix. The comparatively low level of salt is designed to balance well with the bacon or any other well-seasoned filling, so if you're going to eat it plain and hot from the oven, which we heartily recommend, spread thickly with salted butter.

Makes 10 baps
330ml hand-hot water, around 37°C
20g sunflower oil
625g strong white flour, plus extra
   for dusting
7g dried active yeast
10g salt

Place the water and oil into the bowl of a stand mixer, then add the flour, yeast and salt, keeping the yeast and salt on opposite sides of the bowl.

Using the dough hook, mix for 5 minutes on the slow setting, then increase to a moderate speed for about 4 minutes, or until the dough is smooth and shiny.

Turn out onto a lightly floured surface and knead gently for a couple of minutes. If the dough is sticking to your hands or the bench, use a little flour, but don't add too much or the baps will be less soft. Dough can smell fear and will stick to you unless you handle it confidently, so let it know who's boss.

Shape the dough into a rough ball, cover with a damp tea towel and let it rest for 20 minutes at room temperature.

Divide the dough into ten 100g pieces. Shape these pieces into balls on a lightly floured surface, then dust lightly with a little more flour. Cover again with a damp tea towel and rest for another 10–15 minutes at room temperature.

Line two metal baking sheets with baking parchment.

Squish the balls out a little into ovals, from the middle outwards, using a rolling pin with gentle pressure, until each ball is about 8cm across, then place onto the baking sheets.

Cover with a damp tea towel and leave in a warm room for 45 minutes until doubled in size.

Bake at 235°C (215°C fan) for 8–10 minutes until they have a very light golden colour.

Super seedy baps

We make some astonishingly beautiful artisanal loaves in the Fitzbillies bakery – big, crisp, crusty beauties – but our bestselling bread is by far a much more idiosyncratic creation. The people of Cambridge go crazy for super seedy baps. Odd things, they are flattish, soft with a light brown crust, but loaded with a huge amount of mixed seeds and topped with even more. It's a bap with character. It's also, secretly, Tim's favourite task in the bakery… dropping the gently risen dough balls into a huge tray of seed mix with a satisfying 'flump' noise and making sure the maximum number of seeds stick.

Makes 10 baps
315ml hand-hot water, around 37°C
10g sunflower oil, plus extra for oiling
390g strong white flour, plus extra for dusting
130g wholemeal flour
7g dried active yeast
15g salt
140g seed mix, plus a lot extra for dipping
    (we use a roughly equal quantity of
    pumpkin, poppy, sunflower and linseed)

Place the water and oil in the bowl of a stand mixer, then add the flours, yeast and salt, keeping the yeast and salt on opposite sides of the bowl. Using the dough hook, mix for 5 minutes on the slow setting.

Now add the seed mix. Speed the mixer up to a moderate speed for about 5 minutes, or until the dough has come together with the seeds evenly distributed throughout.

Turn the dough out onto a lightly floured surface (try to use very little flour). If the dough is too sticky, rub a small amount of sunflower oil onto your hands. Knead gently for a couple of minutes, shape into a rough ball shape, cover with a damp tea towel and rest for 20 minutes at room temperature.

Divide the dough into ten 100g pieces, then shape into balls on a lightly floured surface. Cover with a damp tea towel and rest for another 10–15 minutes at room temperature until doubled in size. Line two metal baking sheets with baking parchment.

Squish the balls out a little from the middle outwards, using a rolling pin with gentle pressure, until each ball is about 8cm across.

Tip the extra seed mix onto a dinner plate, spray each bap with clean water, then dip into the seed mix. Press down gently to attach as many seeds as you can to the baps, then put the baps onto the baking tray, seed side up.

Cover with a damp tea towel and leave in a warm room for 45 minutes until they have almost doubled in size. Preheat the oven to 230°C (210°C fan).

Spray the baps with a misting of water and bake for 10–12 minutes until they are a very light golden colour. If they are baked for too long, they will be less soft – the lighter the bake, the better the bap.

Index

CAPPUCCINO	3.00	2.75
MOCHA	3.50	3.25
HOT CHOCOLATE	3.50	3.25
AEROPRESS	3.60	3.40
COLD BREW	2.75	2.50
ICED LATTE	3.25	3.00

TEA

FITZBILLIES LOOSE LEAF

AFTERNOON CEYLON , EARL GREY	3.20	
ENGLISH BREAKFAST	3.00	
HERB & FRUIT TEA	3.00	1.80
ICED TEA	2.60	2.20

ICE CREAM

ICE CREAM SUNDAE	6.75
TWO SCOOPS	5.00

★FITZBILLIES VOUCHERS★

£10 £20

Publishing Director Sarah Lavelle
Editor Harriet Webster
Copy Editor Muna Reyal
Designer Will Webb
Photographer Sam A. Harris
Photographer's Assistant Alex Catt
Prop Stylist Faye Wears
Production Director Vincent Smith
Production Controller Nikolaus Ginelli

First published in 2019 by Quadrille,
an imprint of Hardie Grant Publishing

Quadrille
52–54 Southwark Street
London SE1 1UN
quadrille.com

Text © Fitzbillies 2019
Photography © Sam A. Harris 2019
Photo p.9 © Richard Saker/Observer/
eyevine
Photo pp.14–15 © JET Photographic
Photo pp.176–177 © Tim Hayward
Design and layout © Quadrille 2019

Cataloguing in Publication Data:
a catalogue record for this book is
available from the British Library.

ISBN 978 1 78713 523 9

Printed in China

The publisher has made every effort to
trace copyright holders. We apologise in
advance for any unintentional omissions
and would be pleased to insert the
appropriate acknowledgement in
any subsequent edition.